AI's Knowledge Web: Logic Unleashed

Sachin

Contents

Chapter 1

Introduction

Knowledge representation and reasoning (KRR) is the field of logic-based Artificial Intelligence (AI) in which symbolic propositions are interpreted and manipulated in an automated way by reasoning programs [9]. A knowledge base represents a set of facts about some domain, is used to obtain useful information from it that is not explicitly defined and to solve complex decision problems. [28]. KRR seeks to address three main questions:

- How best to represent what we know, i.e., finding an appropriate representation for specific domains so that we do not lose information about the world around us.

- How to use the representation to infer new knowledge, i.e., how can we make use of explicitly defined information to derive implicit information. This question is at the central part of any logic which is often called *entailment*.

- Finally, how to manage the trade-off between expressivity and computational efficiency [2].

To answer these three questions, different forms of logic are used to represent knowledge such as propositional logics, first-order logic (FOL), description logics (DLs) or modal logics. From a computational point of view, it is always advised to select a representation language that is expressive enough to encode what is required and nothing more [2]. Description Logics (DLs) are well-known formalisms for reasoning about information in a given domain. DLs have many advantages such as being decidable fragments of first-order logic, and having a clear semantics and well-defined reasoning procedures which can be automated [2, 27]. We can use the well-defined syntax and semantics of DLs to define entailment which allows us to derive implicit knowledge that can be made explicit through inferences [2].

There are various logic-based reasoning services and corresponding tools in AI. In the case of Description Logics, they are quite efficient and are used to solve problems such as *satisfiability*, i.e., given a description, determine whether it contains any contradictory information, and *subsumption*: determine whether one description is more general than another [25]. Reductions between reasoning services also enable only one reasoning procedure to be implemented which alleviates the need of creating tools to perform each and every reasoning service [45, 48]. Various reasoning techniques/algorithms have been developed to solve some of the reasoning problems highlighted above. The most widely used technique, the tableau-based approach, has been shown to be efficient in practice for real knowledge bases [2].

The DL services mentioned above can be made more useful by adding explanations to the conclusions that DLs systems can draw. Using the example above, the answer to our query "do robins have wings?" was YES. However, it is more beneficial to users if the DL system can also provide an explanation of how it came to the conclusion. In this example an explanation to the query is that "we know that robins are birds, and birds have wings, therefore we can conclude that robins have wings".

Explanation facilities are an essential part of knowledge base development tools. They are useful in understanding entailments, debugging and repairing information declared in knowledge bases and also knowledge base comprehension. For example, given a large knowledge base a user can use explanations to determine which statements are responsible for an entailment without having to understand all the declared statements. In the same way, knowledge base comprehension can be made easier with explanations especially in cases where the user is faced with a knowledge base they have not seen before. Furthermore, when a knowledge base entails information that is incoherent, explanations allow the user to pinpoint the statements which are responsible and also helps the user understand why the undesirable conclusion was drawn. Thus explanations can help the user to repair the knowledge base to a consistent state [26].

In our example above, our knowledge base is very small with only five statements. In reality knowledge bases can contain ten of thousands of statements and without automated support for explanation, it can be difficult to identify the statements that give rise to certain entailments [5, 26]. As a result, there are various algorithms to compute justifications, and implementations of these algorithms for the DL case are available through the ontology editor Protégé [26].

Despite the definitions of classical logic such as propositional logics which help provide an accurate description of the domain, they do not allow for any exceptions within a knowledge base. This is because classical logics are monotonic, which means that the addition of any new explicit information in a knowledge base should never remove an inference entailed from the knowledge base.

For this reason, defeasible reasoning extends classical logic by introducing well defined and systematic approaches to exceptions to general rules [50]. One such approach is the Kraus,Lehmann, and Magidor (KLM) approach to defeasible reasoning, which was originally defined for propositional logic, but has been lifted to the case for DLs [15]. This is done by introducing the notion of defeasibility, that is, statements that present a typical rather than direct logical dependency [18]. In a defeasible logic, typicality allows for reasoning about logical statements that would otherwise conflict with each other. Rational closure is a specific method within the KLM approach that has a well-defined semantics [11] and an implementation [38] for the ontology editor Protégé . See Figure 1.1 for an overview structure and where it is categorised.

The rational closure algorithm performs reasoning by first constructing a ranking where every defeasible statement has a rank [11]. A defeasible statement is exceptional if its antecedent is exceptional with respect to the knowledge base. In order to determine the rank of a statement, you first have to check how exceptional it is.

Let us extend the example above to the defeasible case. Suppose the knowledge

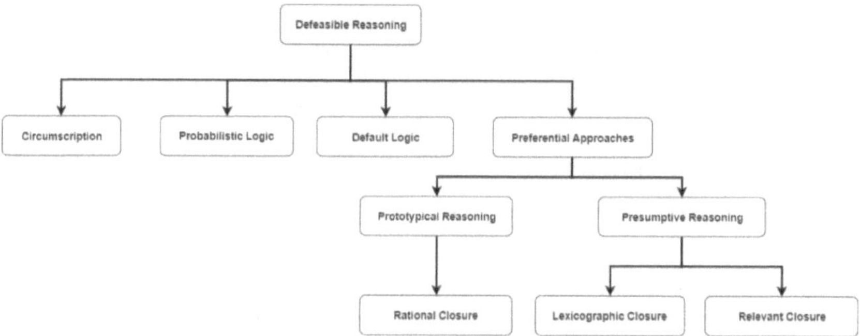

Figure 1.1: Defeasible Reasoning Overview

base contains the following the statements: "penguins are birds", "robins are birds", "penguins do not fly", "birds typically fly" and "birds typically have wings".

When we query this knowledge base and ask "do penguins typically have wings", the answer to the query using rational closure is NO. The reason the system returns NO is not as straightforward as one might think. The issue is that if a typical thing has some properties such as birds having wings, and if we have a subclass of birds such as robins or penguins, do they inherit the properties of the super-class? That is dependent on how you look at things, for example if it is a typical bird such as a robin, then it probably inherits all the properties but if it is an atypical bird such as a penguin then maybe it does not inherit all the properties of being a bird. Initially, a user might use the same arguments that were used in our initial version of our example but that justification leads to errors. Thus, it is useful if defeasible reasoning is extended to include explanations.

In this work, we combine explanations with defeasible reasoning. Generally, when you look at classical DLs, the explanations can be derived from using DL reasoning services. But here we need to take defeasibility into account, and the way in which the explanations are obtained are more complex because we have to consider the ranking of statements.

For instance, in order to obtain the explanation to the query "do penguins have wings", we first look at all justifications that support the answer YES. The statements "penguins are birds" and "birds typically have wings" can be used to justify the answer. However, according to the information in our knowledge base we know that penguins can not fly thus the logical consequence of this is that there are no penguins since the existence of penguins will cause a conflict. As a result using rational closure, the statements "birds typically fly" and "birds typically have wings" are discarded meaning we can no longer use them in our justification, thus giving the explanation of why the answer to the query is NO.

Generally from an algorithmic perspective what is happening is if the answer to a query is YES, look at all the minimal sets which include only the statements required for the entailment to hold. Then check for the ones that occur as part of the ranked statements. That will be the real explanation. However, note that an entailment can have more than one justification and other justifications can be used to build up the explanation. If the answer is NO, then check to see if there are any minimal subsets that entail the negation [3] of the query and build the explanation from there which is how we came up with the explanation for the query above. Thus, looking at the example above it is clear that explanation for defeasible reasoning will have the same advantages explanation has for classical reasoning systems.

1.1   Motivation

The motivation of this book is that it has already been established that explanation for classical reasoning is a useful service.

Consider the example extended to the defeasible case above. The query "do penguins typically have wings" requires a more complicated explanation because it is plausible to conclude that indeed penguins have wings.

Looking at this simple example NO is the correct answer but simply saying NO is not enough and more information is required in form of an explanation in order to understand how we came up with the answer.

Thus, it is clear that explanation for defeasible reasoning would be a good service for the same reasons as the classical reasoning case. Additionally, to the best of our knowledge there has been little research that has gone into extending explanations for defeasible reasoning. The only work found similar to our research is provided by Brewka and Ulbricht [10] which focuses on one nonmonotonic formalism, namely logic programs under answer set semantics specifically looking at propositional programs which they refer to as "strong explanations". Brewka and Ulbricht [10] discuss some consequences of strong explanations for description logics and make the claim that strong explanations can be generalized to arbitrary monotonic and nonmonotonic logics.

1.2   Problem Statement

Understanding the conclusions drawn from logic-based systems are complex and requires expert knowledge especially when defeasible knowledge bases are taken into account for both expert and general users. Simply providing or listing the statements that are responsible for an entailment in the classical case is enough to justify an entailment. However, when looking at the defeasible case this is not adequate because the way in which entailment is performed is more complicated than the classical case.

1.3   Contribution

In this book we focus on one approach to defeasible reasoning, i.e., Rational Closure [11] and extend it with explanations. We provide a theoretical framework for explanation for defeasible reasoning.

1.4   book Outline

The book is structured as follows:

Chapter 2 introduces the basic background to the Description Logic $\mathcal{ALC}$. The chapter focuses on the concepts, definitions and terminology used throughout this book.

Chapter 3 uses the foundations outlined in Chapter 2 and introduces justification-based explanations. A background to justifications and formal definitions are provided. The chapter concludes with a section on advancing justifications with translating them to English expressions.

Chapter 4 introduces defeasible reasoning. Specifically, we examine rational closure which is a preferential approach that allows the representation of information that would otherwise conflict with each other.

The main contribution of this **book** is in Chapter 5. In this chapter we present the algorithm to compute justification for defeasible reasoning.

Chapter 6 summarizes the dissertation's contribution, and ends with some future work.

Chapter 2

Description Logics

This chapter introduce Description Logics (DLs). First we give the syntax and semantics of DLs. Second we discuss entailment and lastly, we conclude the chapter with an overview of common reasoning services for DLs.

2.1   Background

Description logics (DLs) form a large family of logic-based knowledge representation formalisms that are decidable fragments of first-order Logic. DLs are well-suited to represent the conceptual knowledge of an application domain in a structured and formally well-understood way [12].

DLs are employed in various application domains, such as natural language processing, configurations, terminological knowledge, database schemata, evolution, query optimisation and bio-medical ontologies. However, their most notable success so far is the adoption of the DL-based language (OWL) Web Ontology Language as a standard ontology language for the semantic web [2, 4, 27].

Description logics are mainly characterised by a set of constructors that describe a domain of interest in terms of:

- *Concepts* - which represent the basic classes of a domain, e.g. Person

- *Roles* - also called relations or properties, e.g. hasChild

- *Individuals* - names of objects in the domain, e.g. john

At the core of each description logic is a *concept language*. The concept language is a formal language which allows us to build concept descriptions and role descriptions from concept names, role names, and possibly other primitives [2]. For example, $\exists$hasChild.Male is such a concept description built from the concept names Male and role name hasChild which represents individuals that have at least one child who is male. The concept language also determines the expressivity of the description logic, which is defined by allowing or disallowing different constructors e.g. conjunction, disjunction, negation and quantifiers in their language. Additionally, the expressiveness of a description logic affects the complexity of reasoning for this description logic.

In this work, we are primarily interested in the description logic $\mathcal{ALC}$ because defeasible reasoning for $\mathcal{ALC}$ has been studied and implemented [39]. Additionally,

$\mathcal{ALC}$ can arguably be considered as the representative DL which means that most research starts with $\mathcal{ALC}$ and if it works then extensions can be made for more expressive DLs .

The remainder of this chapter is organized as follows. Section 2.2 introduces the syntax and semantics of the basic Description Logic $\mathcal{ALC}$. We provide a detailed description of entailment in this section as it is the main focus when looking at providing explanations for defeasible $\mathcal{ALC}$. We conclude the chapter by briefly discussing some of the popular reasoning services provided by DLs in Section 2.3 .

2.2   The Description Logic $\mathcal{ALC}$

The logic we are going to look at is called $\mathcal{ALC}$ and it stands for Attributive (Concept) Language with Complements. It includes concept names, concept intersection, concept union, complement, existential and universal quantifiers, and individual names. The following section provides the syntax and semantics of the DL $\mathcal{ALC}$ as well as important definitions that will be used throughout the rest of the book.

Definition 1 (Syntax) The vocabulary consists of three disjoint alphabets of symbols: atomic concepts, atomic roles and individuals.

Complex descriptions can be built from them inductively with concept constructors and role constructors. Concept descriptions in $\mathcal{ALC}$ are formed according to the following syntax rule:

$$
\begin{aligned}
C, D ::= \ &A &&\text{Atomic concept} \\
&\top &&\text{Universal concept} \\
&\bot &&\text{Bottom concept} \\
&\neg C &&\text{Negation} \\
&C \sqcup D &&\text{Union} \\
&C \sqcap D &&\text{Intersection} \\
&\exists R.C &&\text{Existential restriction} \\
&\forall R.C &&\text{Universal restriction}
\end{aligned}
$$

where A is an atomic concept, C and D are concept descriptions, and R is a role name. Every concept name is an $\mathcal{ALC}$ concept description, so are $\bot$ and $\top$ and so are the others ($C \sqcup D$, $C \sqcap D$, $\exists R.C$ and $\forall R.C$).

The following are examples of:

- Atomic concepts: Person, Father, Male, Female

- Atomic roles: hasChild, marriedTo

- Complex descriptions: $\exists$hasChild.Male, Female $\sqcup$ Male, Person $\sqcap$ $\neg$Female

Definition 2 (Semantics) Description logic complex descriptions are given a semantics by introducing the notion of *interpretations*. An interpretation is a structure $\mathcal{I}$ $= \langle\, \Delta^{\mathcal{I}}, \cdot^{\mathcal{I}} \,\rangle$ where $\Delta^{\mathcal{I}}$ is a non-empty set called the domain, and $\cdot^{\mathcal{I}}$ is an interpretation function mapping concept names A to subsets $A^{\mathcal{I}}$ of $\Delta^{\mathcal{I}}$, and mapping role names R to binary relations $R^{\mathcal{I}}$ over $\Delta^{\mathcal{I}} \times \Delta^{\mathcal{I}}$.

This means concepts are interpreted as subsets of the domain; role names are interpreted as binary relations over the domain and individuals are mapped to elements of the domain. The intuition is that it gives a complete description of the world and what it means is that the moment we have an interpretation $\mathcal{I}$ the only things we can talk about are the elements in my domain. Specifically, for all those elements we know which concepts they belong to and also exactly how they are related to each other via role names and from that information we can build complex descriptions.

The interpretation function is extended to concept descriptions by the following inductive definitions:

$$
\begin{aligned}
\top^{\mathcal{I}} &= \Delta^{\mathcal{I}} \\
\bot^{\mathcal{I}} &= \emptyset \\
\neg C &= \Delta^{\mathcal{I}} \setminus C^{\mathcal{I}} \\
(C \sqcup D)^{\mathcal{I}} &= C^{\mathcal{I}} \cup D^{\mathcal{I}} \\
(C \sqcap D)^{\mathcal{I}} &= C^{\mathcal{I}} \cap D^{\mathcal{I}} \\
(\exists R.C)^{\mathcal{I}} &= \{a \in \Delta^{\mathcal{I}} \mid \text{There is a } b \in \Delta^{\mathcal{I}} \text{ s.t. } (a,b) \in R^{\mathcal{I}} \text{ and } b \in C^{\mathcal{I}} \} \\
(\forall R.C)^{\mathcal{I}} &= \{a \in \Delta^{\mathcal{I}} \mid \text{For all } b \in \Delta^{\mathcal{I}}, \text{ if } (a,b) \in R^{\mathcal{I}} \text{ then } b \in C^{\mathcal{I}} \}
\end{aligned}
$$

For example, the concept Male is intended to be the set of male persons. The complex concept Person $\sqcap \neg$Female represents the set of individuals that are persons and are not female. Similarly $\exists$hasChild.Male represents the set of individuals that have at least one child who is a male.

In DL, a clear distinction is drawn between the so-called TBox (Terminological Box) and the ABox (Assertional Box). A TBox introduces the terminology and an ABox contains facts about particular objects in the application domain. Together ABox and TBox statements make up a knowledge base. Unlike a database, a DL knowledge base does not fully describe a particular situation or "state of the world". Instead, it consists of a set of statements called axioms, each of which must be true in the situation described. These axioms typically capture only partial information about the situation that the knowledge base is describing, and there may be many different interpretations that are consistent with the knowledge base [33].

We now define what a TBox, ABox and knowledge base are.

Definition 3 (TBox) Let C and D be complex concepts. A TBox $\mathcal{T}$ is a finite collection of:

- *General Concept Inclusion* (GCI) axioms or *subsumption statements* of the form $C \sqsubseteq D$, read as "C is subsumed by D". The intuition is "C is more specific than D (or D is more general than C).

  For example, Father $\sqsubseteq$ Parent and Man $\sqsubseteq$ Male $\sqcup$ Person

- *Concept Equivalence* axioms of the form $C \equiv D$, read as "C is equivalent to D", which is an abbreviation for both $C \sqsubseteq D$ and $D \sqsubseteq C$.

  For example, Grandparent $\equiv \exists$hasChild.Parent

The semantics of TBox statements is as follows. An interpretation $\mathcal{I}$ is a model of a GCI $C \sqsubseteq D$ (denoted $\mathcal{I} \Vdash C \sqsubseteq D$) if $C^{\mathcal{I}} \subseteq D^{\mathcal{I}}$, and it satisfies a concept equivalence $C \equiv D$ (denoted $\mathcal{I} \Vdash C \equiv D$) if and only if $C^{\mathcal{I}} = D^{\mathcal{I}}$. $\mathcal{I}$ is a model of a TBox $\mathcal{T}$ if it is a model of every GCI in $\mathcal{T}$.

In the TBox, one defines concepts of the application domain, their properties and their relations.

Definition 4 (ABox) Let C be a concept description, R a role name, and a and b individual names. An ABox $\mathcal{A}$ is a set of assertions about individuals. Objects in the ABox are referred to by a finite number of individual names, and these names may be used in two types of assertional statements:

- Concept assertions of type $C(a)$ i.e., a belongs to (the interpretation of) C.

  For example, Man(john), and Woman(mary) which assert that john is a man and mary is a woman.

- Role assertions of the type $R(a, b)$ i.e., b is a filler of the role R for a. Role fillers distinguish the function of concepts in a relationship [48]

  For example, marriedTo(john, mary) states that mary is married to an individual named john, more precisely the individual named mary (role filler) is in the relation that is represented by marriedTo (role) to the individual named john.

We give a semantics to ABoxes by extending interpretations to individual names. This means that an interpretation $\mathcal{I} = \langle \Delta^{\mathcal{I}}, \cdot^{\mathcal{I}} \rangle$ not only maps atomic concepts and roles to sets and relations but also maps each individual name a to an element $a^{\mathcal{I}} \in \Delta^{\mathcal{I}}$.

The interpretation $\mathcal{I}$ satisfies the concept assertion $C(a)$ if $a^{\mathcal{I}} \in C^{\mathcal{I}}$, and it satisfies the role assertion $R(a, b)$ if $(a^{\mathcal{I}}, b^{\mathcal{I}}) \in R^{\mathcal{I}}$). An interpretation satisfies the ABox $\mathcal{A}$ if it satisfies each assertion in $\mathcal{A}$.

Definition 5 (Knowledge Base) An $\mathcal{ALC}$ knowledge base $\mathcal{K}$ is a pair $(\mathcal{T}, \mathcal{A})$, where $\mathcal{T}$ is an $\mathcal{ALC}$ TBox and $\mathcal{A}$ is an $\mathcal{ALC}$ ABox. An interpretation $\mathcal{I}$ is a model of a knowledge base $\mathcal{K} = (\mathcal{T}, \mathcal{A})$ (denoted $\mathcal{I} \Vdash \mathcal{K}$) if $\mathcal{I}$ is a model of $\mathcal{T}$ and $\mathcal{I}$ is a model of $\mathcal{A}$

Hence for an interpretation to be a model of $\mathcal{K}$, it has to satisfy all assertions in $\mathcal{K}$'s ABox and all GCIs in $\mathcal{K}$'s TBox. Formally:

- $\mathcal{I} \Vdash \mathcal{T}$ if and only if $\mathcal{I} \Vdash C \sqsubseteq D$ for every $C \sqsubseteq D \in \mathcal{T}$

- $\mathcal{I} \Vdash \mathcal{A}$ if and only if

  - $\mathcal{I} \Vdash C(a)$ for every $C(a) \in \mathcal{A}$, and
  - $\mathcal{I} \Vdash R(a, b)$ for every $R(a, b) \in \mathcal{A}$

- If $\mathcal{I} \Vdash \mathcal{T}$, we say $\mathcal{I}$ is a model of $\mathcal{T}$

- If $\mathcal{I} \Vdash \mathcal{A}$, we say $\mathcal{I}$ is a model of $\mathcal{A}$

- If $\mathcal{I} \Vdash \mathcal{A}$, then $\mathcal{I}$ is a model of $\mathcal{K} = (\mathcal{T}, \mathcal{A})$

For example, we can represent notions of human relations using the following TBox $\mathcal{T}$ and ABox $\mathcal{A}$:

$$\mathcal{T} = \left\{ \begin{array}{c} \text{Woman} \sqsubseteq \neg\text{Man}, \\ \text{Parent} \equiv \exists\text{hasChild}.\top, \\ \top \equiv (\text{Man} \sqcup \text{Woman}) \\ \text{Grandparent} \equiv \exists\text{hasChild}.\text{Parent}, \\ \text{Husband} \sqsubseteq \exists\text{marriedTo}.\text{Woman}, \\ \text{Wife} \sqsubseteq \exists\text{marriedTo}.\text{Man}, \\ \text{Father} \equiv \text{Man} \sqcap \text{Parent}, \\ \text{Mother} \equiv \text{Woman} \sqcap \text{Parent} \end{array} \right\}$$

$$\mathcal{A} = \left\{ \begin{array}{c} \text{Woman}(\text{anne}), \text{Man}(\text{pete}), \\ \text{Woman}(\text{mary}), \text{Man}(\text{john}), \\ \text{Woman}(\text{alice}), \\ \text{marriedTo}(\text{pete}, \text{anne}), \\ \text{marriedTo}(\text{anne}, \text{pete}), \\ \text{marriedTo}(\text{john}, \text{mary}), \\ \text{marriedTo}(\text{mary}, \text{john}), \\ \text{hasChild}(\text{pete}, \text{john}), \\ \text{hasChild}(\text{anne}, \text{john}), \\ \text{hasChild}(\text{john}, \text{alice}) \end{array} \right\}$$

So far we have discussed the syntax and semantics of $\mathcal{ALC}$ description logics. We now build on these foundations by introducing entailment which allows us to derive implicit knowledge that can be made explicit through inferences [2]. Entailment is a basic logic notion that defines the connection between statements that are true if one declaration follows logically from one or more statements.

Using entailment, we can ask the following questions; Given a TBox $\mathcal{T}$, what other subsumptions follow? Given an ABox $\mathcal{A}$, what other assertions follow? Also, given a knowledge base $\mathcal{K} = (\mathcal{T}, \mathcal{A})$, what statements follow from it?

Definition 6 (Entailment)

Given $\mathcal{K} = (\mathcal{T}, \mathcal{A})$ and a statement η, where $\mathcal{T}$ is a TBox, $\mathcal{A}$ is an ABox and η is a TBox statement, entailment is defined by:

- $\mathcal{T} \models \eta$ (read as $\mathcal{T}$ entails η) if and only if, for every $\mathcal{I}$, if $\mathcal{I} \Vdash \mathcal{T}$, then $\mathcal{I} \Vdash \eta$

- $\mathcal{A} \models \eta$ (read as $\mathcal{A}$ entails η) if and only if, for every $\mathcal{I}$, if $\mathcal{I} \Vdash \mathcal{A}$, then $\mathcal{I} \Vdash \eta$

- $\mathcal{K} \models \eta$ (read as $\mathcal{K}$ entails η) if and only if, for every $\mathcal{I}$, if $\mathcal{I} \Vdash \mathcal{K}$, then $\mathcal{I} \Vdash \eta$

Using the knowledge base representing human relations defined above, we can conclude the following entailments.

- $\mathcal{K} \models \text{Mother} \sqcap \text{Wife} \sqsubseteq \exists\text{hasChild}.\top \sqcap \exists\text{marriedTo}.\text{Man}.$

- $\mathcal{K} \models \text{Man} \sqcap \text{Parent}(\text{john}).$

  We know these entailments are true because when we look at the knowledge base and statements, intuitively we can see that the statements hold. But the reason the entailments hold formally is that, if we look at any interpretation $\mathcal{I}$ which makes all of the statements in the knowledge base true, then it is going to make the statements true as well. Verifying whether or not statements are entailed from knowledge bases is tricky, that is why we use reasoning services because they have been proven to be sound and complete which tell us that the reasoning services work as intended . In the same way when we are asked to multiply two large numbers, it will generally take a longer period of time and that is why we use calculators. We trust that when we use the calculator it will produce the intended correct result.

- $\mathcal{K} \not\models$ Grandparent(mary).

  However, the entailment above does not hold. This is because the definition of being a Grandparent requires you have a child who also has a child.

To complete the discussion on DLs, we briefly discuss the different kinds of reasoning services performed by a DL system. Specifically, we discuss reasoning services that are applicable to $\mathcal{ALC}$.

2.3 DL Reasoning Services

The use of explicitly stated information in TBoxes and ABoxes alone does not take advantage of the full potential of DL knowledge bases. Deriving implicit, useful information through reasoning services is essential for performing advanced tasks such as understanding 3D models, indexing and querying [48]. The following is a list of the most basic DL reasoning services:

1. Concept Satisfiability

   Given a TBox $\mathcal{T}$ and a concept C, check whether C is satisfiable w.r.t. $\mathcal{T}$, i.e.,, whether there exists a model $\mathcal{I}$ of $\mathcal{K}$ such that $C^{\mathcal{I}} \neq \emptyset$

2. Subsumption

   Given a TBox $\mathcal{T}$ and two concepts C and D, check whether C is subsumed by D w.r.t. $\mathcal{T}$, i.e.,, whether $C^{\mathcal{I}} \subseteq D^{\mathcal{I}}$ in every model $\mathcal{I}$ of $\mathcal{K}$

3. Consistency Checking

   Given a knowledge base $\mathcal{K} = (\mathcal{T}, \mathcal{A})$, check whether $\mathcal{K}$ is satisfiable, i.e., whether it has a model.

4. Instance Checking

   Given a knowledge base $\mathcal{K} = (\mathcal{T}, \mathcal{A})$, an individual name a, and a concept C, check whether the assertion $C(a)$ is satisfied in every model of $\mathcal{K}$

We saw that entailment is used to infer information from knowledge bases and that reasoning services are used to verify whether or not the statements hold. Recall the entailment $\mathcal{K} \models$ Mother $\sqcap$ Wife $\sqsubseteq \exists$hasChild.$\top \sqcap \exists$marriedTo.Man, this is checked using subsumption; $\mathcal{K} \models$ Man $\sqcap$ Parent(john) is verified using instance checking and $\mathcal{K} \not\models$ Grandparent(mary) is verified using instance checking. In other words, given an entailment, one of the four reasoning services above can be used to verify if the statement holds.

Reductions enable only one reasoning procedure to be implemented which alleviates the need of creating tools to perform each and every reasoning service [45].

Concept satisfiability, subsumption, and instance checking can be reduced to consistency checking or knowledge base satisfiability for all description logics that are closed under negation [48]

Various reasoning techniques and algorithms have been developed to solve some of the reasoning problems highlighted above. These include automata-based approaches, resolution and consequence-based approaches, query rewriting approaches and the most widely used technique, tableau-based approach [2].

Tableau-based algorithms for $\mathcal{ALC}$ have been shown to be efficient because they terminate, are complete and sound for real knowledge bases, even if the problem in the corresponding logic is in PSPACE or EXPTIME [2]. We end our discussion on DLs with the reasoning services because when generating justifications for an entailment (which we are going to discuss in the next chapter) we use some of the reasoning services such as consistency checking and satisfiability.

2.4   Summary

This chapter has introduced the basic Description Logic $\mathcal{ALC}$ for knowledge representation. We provided the syntax, semantics and discussed how entailment (logical consequence) can be used to derive implicit information from our knowledge base. Finally, DL reasoning services were highlighted.

In the next chapter we discuss justifications and how useful they are in terms of understanding entailments that are derived from a knowledge base. Once we have done this we then address the issue of handling exceptions in $\mathcal{ALC}$ knowledge bases in Chapter 4.

Chapter 3

Justification-Based Explanation

In this chapter we build on the foundations of description logics introduced in Chapter 2 with explanations. We specifically look at explanations for description logic knowledge bases. Note that literature usually refers to ontologies to describe information in a domain but Chapter 2, shows that we can use description logics to represent information in a domain through a knowledge base. Therefore, to maintain consistency, we will use the term knowledge base in the remainder of this book denoted by $(\mathcal{K})$ to refer to an ontology. An ontology is a computer-processable artefact representing information about the entities in a domain, and the relationships between them [26].

The field of explanation explores why selected consequences are derivable from an ontology. For example, an ontology may contain a class named 'Bird', described as a sub-class of 'Animal' with distinguishing properties such as birds that have 'flight' capabilities, have wings and feathers such as robins, and also birds that have wings and feathers but can not fly such as chickens or ostriches and also those birds that do not have 'flight' capabilities such as penguins. Using a formal logic-based language such as descriptions logics, information about the world can be represented in an ontology. The expressiveness of DLs and decidability property make DLs a good logical foundation of ontology languages [40]. Recall from Chapter 2 that description logics are mainly characterised by a set of constructors that describe a domain of interest in terms of concepts, roles and individuals which are synonymous to classes, object and data properties and individuals for an ontology.

In Section 3.1 we give a background to explanation and then introduce the necessary foundations for justifications in Section 3.2. In Section 3.3 we discuss various techniques for computing justifications. Section 3.4 gives a detailed description of the algorithm used to compute justification. Finally, we conclude the chapter with a section that discusses the use of justifications and how to express them in natural language for easy readability.

3.1   Background

Entailment allows users to derive useful implicit information that can be made explicit through inferences which we showed in Chapter 2. However, it is more beneficial to users if the DL system can also provide an explanation of how it came to the conclusion. Take the well-known penguin example [36], and consider a knowledge base containing the statements: "penguins are birds", "robins are birds", "penguins do not fly", "birds fly" and "birds have wings". Using this information we can query the knowledge base, ask "do robins have wings", and the answer would be YES. In this example the explanation to the query could be that "we know that robins are birds, and birds have wings, therefore we can conclude that robins have wings". In this book we focus only on the minimal subsets that entails the conclusion to provide explanations. However, we acknowledge that in order to build sophisticated explanation tools we need to do more than just computing a single justification and presenting it to the user. Considerations such as selecting an explanation when there are more than one and also ensuring that the explanation chosen is more understandable than the rest needs to be taken into account [40].

Explanation facilities are useful in understanding entailments, debugging and repairing information declared in knowledge bases and also knowledge base comprehension. In our example above our knowledge base is very small with only five statements. In reality knowledge bases can contain tens of thousand of statements and without automated support for explanation, it can be difficult to identify the statements that give rise to entailments [5, 26].

3.2   Justification for Entailments

DLs offer users a wide range of constructors for modelling domain knowledge that can be made useful through the reasoning services. However, the expressivity that DLs offer can be misinterpreted by users and may lead to undesired side-effects. Knowledge base errors such as inconsistencies, incorrect entailments and missing entailments need to be fixed to be able to infer meaningful information from the knowledge base. If errors are not detected and repaired, it renders the knowledge base useless [5, 40]. The debugging stage includes identifying the knowledge base error (e.g. an incorrect entailment), locating the source of the error, and finally repairing the knowledge base by changing or removing (some of) the incorrect information. The goal of debugging is to lose as little of the correct information as possible when making modifications. However, the size and complexity of knowledge bases in reality do not favour manual debugging, thus most reasoners now provide some form of debugging support for entailment [5].

Justifications are the most common form of debugging support that are based on Minimal Unsatisfiability Preserving Sub-TBoxes (MUPS) [47]. The intuition of a justification is to only highlight (pinpoint) the axioms or statements within the knowledge base that are causing errors rather than manually searching the entire knowledge base.

A justification $\mathcal{J}$ for an entailment η in a knowledge base $\mathcal{K}$ is a minimal subset of the knowledge base $\mathcal{K}$ that is sufficient for the entailment η to hold [5, 26, 40]. More precisely,

Definition 7 (Justification [26]). Let $\mathcal{K}$ be a knowledge base and η a TBox subsumption statement. $\mathcal{J}$ is a justification for $\mathcal{K} \models \eta$ if $\mathcal{J} \subseteq \mathcal{K}$; $\mathcal{J} \models \eta$ and, for all $\mathcal{J}' \subset \mathcal{J}$, it holds that $\mathcal{J}' \not\models \eta$.

As we have seen in the definition a justification $\mathcal{J}$ is always relative to an entailment η. We shall use the tuple $(\mathcal{J}, \eta)$ as shorthand to refer to a justification with respect to a single entailment η.

Example 1 Consider the following classic penguin example. Given $\mathcal{K} = (\mathcal{T}, \emptyset)$

$$\mathcal{T} = \left\{ \begin{array}{l} \text{Bird} \sqsubseteq \text{Fly}, \\ \text{Bird} \sqsubseteq \text{Wings}, \\ \text{Penguin} \sqsubseteq \neg\text{Fly}, \\ \text{Penguin} \sqsubseteq \text{Bird}, \\ \text{Robin} \sqsubseteq \text{Bird} \end{array} \right\}$$

The following axiom set is a justification for $\mathcal{K} \models \text{Robin} \sqsubseteq \text{Wings}$:

$$\mathcal{J} = \{\text{Robin} \sqsubseteq \text{Bird}, \text{Bird} \sqsubseteq \text{Wings}\}$$

Figure 3.1 illustrates how a justification for an entailment is linked to axioms in the knowledge base.

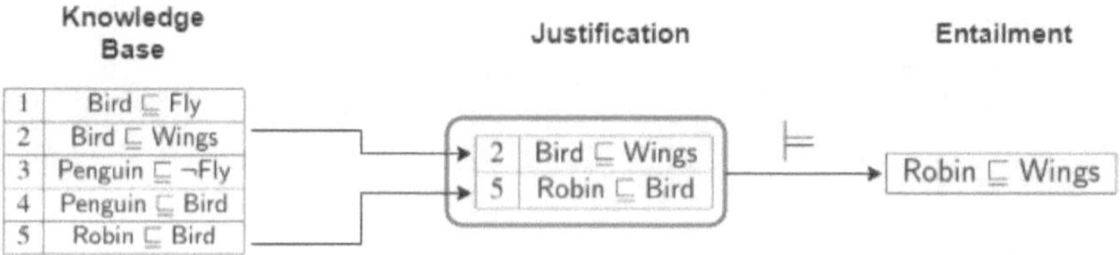

Figure 3.1: Single justification for an entailment

The minimal subset requirement implies that the entailment will no longer be inferable if any axiom is excluded from the justification [5, 26, 29, 40]. For example if axiom number (2) in Figure 3.1 is removed from the justification, the remaining axioms no longer support the entailment $\text{Robin} \sqsubseteq \text{Wings}$. Additionally, the example above only shows one justification but note that depending on the knowledge base, a given entailment may have more than one justification [5, 26, 29, 40]

Example 2 Let us extend the example above with more information about birds and include a special penguin that has flying capabilities. Given $\mathcal{K} = (\mathcal{T}, \emptyset)$

$$\mathcal{T} = \left\{ \begin{array}{l} \text{Bird} \sqsubseteq \text{Fly}, \\ \text{Bird} \sqsubseteq \text{Wings}, \\ \text{Penguin} \sqsubseteq \neg\text{Fly}, \\ \text{SpecialPenguin} \sqsubseteq \text{Fly}, \\ \text{Penguin} \sqsubseteq \text{Bird}, \\ \text{SpecialPenguin} \sqsubseteq \text{Penguin}, \\ \text{Robin} \sqsubseteq \text{Bird} \end{array} \right\}$$

The following two axiom sets $\mathcal{J}_1$ and $\mathcal{J}_2$ are justifications for $\mathcal{K} \models \text{SpecialPenguin} \sqsubseteq \text{Fly}$:

$$\mathcal{J}_1 = \{\text{SpecialPenguin} \sqsubseteq \text{Fly}\}$$
$$\mathcal{J}_2 = \{\text{SpecialPenguin} \sqsubseteq \text{Penguin}, \text{Penguin} \sqsubseteq \text{Bird}, \text{Bird} \sqsubseteq \text{Fly}\}$$

Figure 3.2 shows two justifications $\mathcal{J}_1$ and $\mathcal{J}_2$ for the entailment SpecialPenguin $\sqsubseteq$ Fly. Just like Example 1 if any axiom is removed from the justification set, we can no longer prove that the entailment SpecialPenguin $\sqsubseteq$ Fly holds. Note that when we investigate the knowledge base, justifications $\mathcal{J}_1$ and $\mathcal{J}_2$ in Example 2, the concept is unsatisfiable. Specifically, we have been told that special penguins fly which is a sub-class of penguins that do not fly. Meaning, it is logical to conclude that special penguins will inherit all of penguins attributes as well as including the fact that they cannot fly. However, we have been explicitly told that special penguins have flying capabilities. So do special penguins fly or not? Other than the fact the we have been explicitly told that special penguins fly the way in which to deal with exceptional information requires the introduction of defeasiblity in knowledge bases and also extending classical reasoning services with non-monotonic reasoning features. We discuss defeasible reasoning in greater detail in Chapter 4 and also return to this Example in Chapter 5 and show that generation of explanations through justifications for defeasible knowledge bases is not so straightforward which constitutes the main contribution of the **book**.

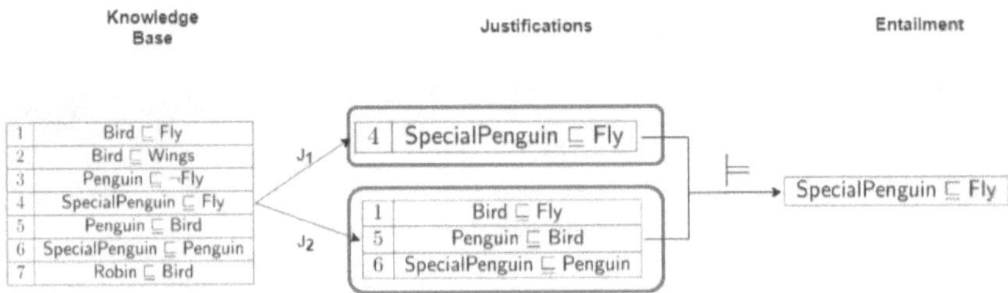

Figure 3.2: Multiple justifications for an entailment

There are various algorithms to compute justifications, and implementations of these algorithms for the DL case are available through the ontology editor Protégé [26] and many more editors such as Swoop, Neologism, TopBraid Composer, Vitro, OWLGrEd and the RaDON plug-in of the NeOn Toolkit [40, 46]. Our focus is on the implementation provided through Protégé [26] because an implementation for defeasible reasoning is available in it.

3.3   Techniques for Computing Justifications

Before we discuss the justification algorithm in detail, let us briefly look at the classification of justification algorithms. Generally algorithms for computing justifications are classified into two main categories, computing a single or all of the available justifications or using a black-box or glass-box approach:

- *Single-All-axis* describe the set of algorithms that either compute a single justification for a given entailment or all possible justifications. Single justification algorithms are usually used as sub-routines in *all* justification algorithms and also assist users in debugging errors, which is why it is of importance to still compute single justifications [5, 26].

- *Reasoner-coupling-axis* describe the set of algorithms that are either a black-box algorithm or a glass-box algorithm. With a black-box approach, a wrapper is built around a standard classical reasoner to compute justifications. The main advantage of this approach is that no prior knowledge of the internal implementation of the reasoner is required and the wrapper stays the same when a better reasoner or alternative logic is used. On the other hand a glass-box approach uses existing standard reasoners and manipulates the internal structure by embedding the code to compute justifications within the reasoner. The main disadvantage with this approach is that it is frequently time consuming and effort required to understand and implement the glass-box algorithm does not outweigh the option of using the black-box approach. The difference between the two mainly stems from the role played by the reasoning procedures, that is whether the justification algorithms are tightly coupled in the reasoning procedures (glass-box) or loosely coupled (black-box) [5, 26, 40].

Regarding the performance and efficiency of justification algorithms, it was found that glass-box algorithms for identifying only a single justification are more efficient than black-box algorithms mainly because the generation of justifications are a by-product of the classification reasoning procedure [5]. However, most implementations to compute justifications fall under the black-box category or a hybrid (black-box glass-box) mainly because of the large amount of work that needs to be done in terms of modifying existing reasoning procedures to incorporate justifications.

3.4   Justification Finding Algorithms

In this section we discuss the algorithm to compute justifications from a knowledge base.

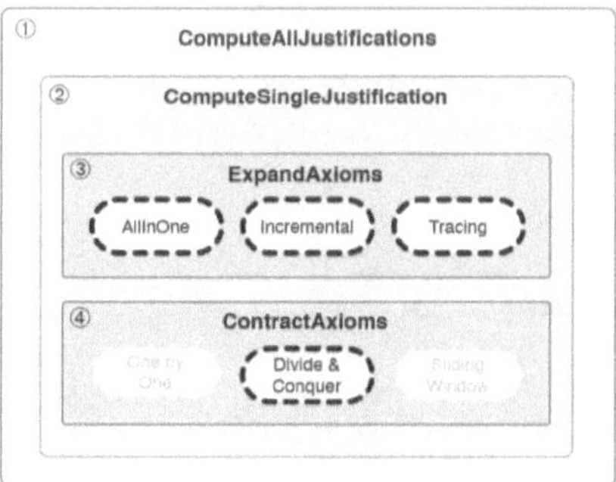

Figure 3.3: Justification Finding Algorithm Topology [26]

Figure 3.3 shows how each of the algorithms are combined to compute justifications. Additionally, Figure 3.3 also shows three different approaches to implement the ExpandAxioms and ContractAxioms algorithms. In this book we only focus on the Incremental approach of the ExpandAxioms algorithm because it is the most comprehensive of the approaches. We also discuss the Divide and Conquer approach of the ContractAxioms algorithm because it has proved to be more efficient than the others [26]. We first discuss the algorithm to compute all justifications because the others are used as sub-routines and will be discussed individually afterwards.

3.4.1   Computing All Justifications for $\mathcal{K} \models \eta$

Algorithm 1: ComputeAllJustifications($\mathcal{K}, \eta$)

Input: Knowledge base $\mathcal{K}$ and entailment η
Output: Set of Justifications $\mathcal{J}$

1   $S_{working} \leftarrow$ ComputeModule($\mathcal{K}, signature(\eta)$)
2   $X_{explored} \leftarrow \emptyset$
3   $X_{result} \quad \emptyset$
4   $J_{root} \leftarrow$ ComputeSingleJustification($S_{working}, \eta$)
5   $X_{result} \leftarrow X_{result} \cup \{J_{root}\}$
6   $v_{root} \leftarrow$ GetFreshNode(J_{root})
7   Enqueue(v_{root}, Q)
8   SetRoot(T_{hst}, v_{root})
9   **while** Q *is not empty* **do**
10     $v_{head} \leftarrow$ Dequeue(Q)
11     $j_{head} \leftarrow$ GetLabel(v_{head})
12   **for** $\alpha \in J_{head}$ **do**
13        $S_{path} \quad$ GetPathToRootLabelSet(v_{head}, T_{hst}) $\cup \{\alpha\}$
14   **if** $S_{path} \notin X_{explored}$ **then**
15           $X_{explored} \quad X_{explored} \cup \{S_{path}\}$
16           $J' \leftarrow$ GetNonIntersectingJustification(S_{path}, X_{result})
17   **if** $J' = \emptyset$ **then**
18              $S_{working} \leftarrow S_{working} \backslash \{S_{path}\}$
19              $J' \leftarrow$ ComputeSingleJustification($S_{working}, \eta$)
20              $S_{working} \quad S_{working} \cup \{S_{path}\}$
21           $v_{fresh} \quad$ GetFreshNode(J')
22           $e \leftarrow$ GetFreshEdge($\langle v_{fresh}, v_{head} \rangle, \alpha$)
23           $T_{hst} \leftarrow T_{hst} \cup \{e\}$
24   **if** $J' \neq \emptyset$ **then**
25              $X_{result} \quad X_{result} \cup \{J'\}$
26   Enqueue(v_{fresh}, Q)

27 **return** X_{result}

The algorithm to compute all justifications for an entailment $\mathcal{K} \models \eta$ uses a hitting set tree T_{hst}. The tree is constructed in a breadth first manner by using a queue Q to store all the justifications as they are computed. Note that a node v represents a justification and an edge e represents an axiom from the knowledge base. The queue function Enqueue(v, Q) adds a node v to the end of a queue Q and the function Dequeue(v, Q) removes a node v from the front of the queue Q. Given $\mathcal{K} \models \eta$, a hitting set tree for η in $\mathcal{K}$ is a finite tree, an example of which is shown in Figure 3.4

The basic procedure is as follows: compute a random justification $\mathcal{J}$ for the entailment η using the algorithm to compute a single justification. Then each axiom α in $\mathcal{J}$ is removed individually from $\mathcal{K}$ resulting in a new knowledge base $\mathcal{K}' = \mathcal{K} \backslash \alpha$. The new knowledge base $\mathcal{K}'$ is then used to compute a new justification without the axiom that was just removed. In order to make the algorithm more concrete let us use Example 2 as our knowledge base and the entailment $\eta = \mathsf{SpecialPenguin} \sqsubseteq \mathsf{Fly}$ to compute its corresponding justifications.

Algorithm 1 to compute all justifications was proposed by Horridge [26].

1. The algorithm begins by extracting a module for the entailment, which is used to initialise a set $S_{working}$ of working axioms. In the most general sense, a module of a knowledge base $\mathcal{K}$ is simply a well defined subset of $\mathcal{K}$ that has some desirable properties [26]. If $\mathcal{K}$ is inconsistent $\mathsf{ComputeModule}$ returns the whole knowledge base and assigns it to $S_{working}$. In line 2 $X_{explored}$ which stores the explored paths of the tree is initialised to an empty set and X_{result} (line 3) which stores the nodes (justifications) is also initialised to an empty set.

   - $S_{working} = \mathcal{K}$
   - $X_{explored} = \emptyset$
   - $X_{result} = \emptyset$

2. In lines 4-8 the algorithm computes a single justification for the entailment η by calling the $\mathsf{ComputeSingleJustification}$ sub-routine and adds this justification to the results set X_{result}. A node is created and assigned to v_{root} by calling the $\mathsf{GetFreshNode}$ function and then initialises the root of the hitting set tree T_{hst} with a node v_{root} which is labelled with this justification. In Figure 3.4 it is labelled as $J_1 = \{\mathsf{SpecialPenguin} \sqsubseteq \mathsf{Fly}\}$.

3. The root node v_{root} which is J_1 is then added to the queue Q to start the construction of the hitting set tree, which takes place in lines 9-27.

   - $S_{working} = \mathcal{K}$
   - $X_{explored} = \emptyset$
   - $X_{result} = \{\mathsf{SpecialPenguin} \sqsubseteq \mathsf{Fly}\}$
   - $v_{root} = \mathsf{SpecialPenguin} \sqsubseteq \mathsf{Fly}$
   - $T_{hst} = \mathsf{SpecialPenguin} \sqsubseteq \mathsf{Fly}$
   - $Q = \mathsf{SpecialPenguin} \sqsubseteq \mathsf{Fly}$

4. To construct the hitting tree we use the current elements in our queue $Q = \mathsf{SpecialPenguin} \sqsubseteq \mathsf{Fly}$ and loop until it is empty. First, select an axiom α that is in the label of v_{head}. Since we only have one axiom in our example, α is assigned $\mathsf{SpecialPenguin} \sqsubseteq \mathsf{Fly}$ and the for loop in line 12 executes. Axioms that get to the root are assigned to S_{path} using the $\mathsf{GetPathToRootLabelSet}$ function in line 13. If the path has not been explored we add the axiom to $X_{explored}$ and then try to find more justifications that do not intersect the current path using the $\mathsf{GetNonIntersectingJustification}$ function.

- $S_{working} = \mathcal{K}$

- $X_{explored} = \mathsf{SpecialPenguin} \sqsubseteq \mathsf{Fly}$

- $X_{result} = \{\mathsf{SpecialPenguin} \sqsubseteq \mathsf{Fly}\}$

- $v_{root} = \mathsf{SpecialPenguin} \sqsubseteq \mathsf{Fly}$

- $T_{hst} = \mathsf{SpecialPenguin} \sqsubseteq \mathsf{Fly}$

- $Q = \mathsf{SpecialPenguin} \sqsubseteq \mathsf{Fly}$

- $S_{path} = \{\mathsf{SpecialPenguin} \sqsubseteq \mathsf{Fly}\}$

5. In lines 17-20 we compute the next justification. If J' is an empty set, remove the axioms in S_{path} from $S_{working}$ to get the new "working axioms" or $\mathcal{K}'$. Next we compute a justification based on our new knowledge base (newly assigned $S_{working}$).

6. Next we create a new node to represent another justification and its corresponding edge. In Figure 3.4 it is labelled as $J_2 = \{\mathsf{SpecialPenguin} \sqsubseteq \mathsf{Penguin}, \mathsf{Penguin} \sqsubseteq \mathsf{Bird}, \mathsf{Bird} \sqsubseteq \mathsf{Fly}\}$. The edge to get from v_{head} to v_{fresh} is created in line 22 via α and added to the hitting set tree T_{hst} in line 23.

7. Lines 24-26 adds the newly created justification J' to the result set X_{result} by checking to see if J' is empty. If not, the new justification is added and the new node v_{root} to the queue Q.

- $S_{working} = \mathcal{K}$

- $X_{explored} = \mathsf{SpecialPenguin} \sqsubseteq \mathsf{Fly}$

- $X_{result} = \{\mathcal{J}_1, \mathcal{J}_2\}$

- $v_{fresh} = \mathcal{J}_2$

- $T_{hst} = \mathsf{SpecialPenguin} \sqsubseteq \mathsf{Fly}$

- $Q = \mathsf{SpecialPenguin} \sqsubseteq \mathsf{Penguin}, \mathsf{Penguin} \sqsubseteq \mathsf{Bird}, \mathsf{Bird} \sqsubseteq \mathsf{Fly}$

8. Since we only had one element in our node $\mathcal{J}_1$, the for loop terminates and the while loop executes in line 9 and goes through the entire procedure to try and compute a 3rd justification by removing an axiom α from $\mathcal{J}_2$ which is the current element in queue Q.

9. The algorithm finally terminates by checking whether the axioms that label the current path label some other path that has already been explored. If this is the case, then early termination is applied to the current path.

10. Finally, the algorithm returns $X_{result} = \{\mathcal{J}_1, \mathcal{J}_2\}$ as the final justification set.

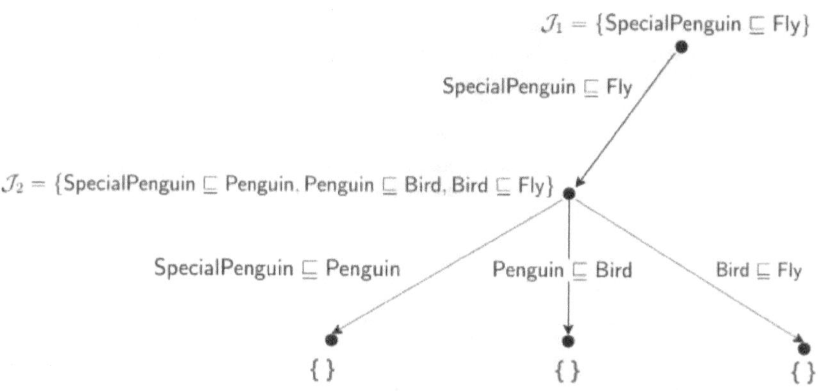

Figure 3.4: An Example of a Hitting Tree

Algorithm 2: ComputeSingleJustification($\mathcal{K}, \eta$)

Input: Knowledge base $\mathcal{K}$ and entailment η
Output: Justification $\mathcal{J}$

1 **if** $\eta \in \mathcal{K}$ **then**
2   ⌊ **return** η
3 S ExpandAxioms($\mathcal{K}, \eta$)
4 **if** $S = \emptyset$ **then**
5   ⌊ **return** $\emptyset$
6 $\mathcal{J} \leftarrow$ ContractAxioms(S, η)
7 **return** $\mathcal{J}$

3.4.2 Computing a Single Justification for $\mathcal{K} \models \eta$

Algorithm 2 to compute a single justification was proposed by Horridge [26].

The ComputeSingleJustification algorithm receives the entire knowledge base $\mathcal{K}$ and entailment η as input and returns a justification $\mathcal{J}$ for the entailment as output. Lines 1-2 are considered as a simple optimisation that returns η if it is a declared statement within the knowledge base as a self-justification Using Example 2 the algorithm will immediately return SpecialPenguin $\sqsubseteq$ Fly as output and terminate because the axiom is already declared in the knowledge base. If lines 1-2 are false the rest of the expand and contract subroutines are executed which are explained in detail in the subsequent sections. Generally, the ExpandAxioms subroutine (line 3) adds axioms to a subset S of $\mathcal{K}$ until it entails η. This creates a superset S' of $\mathcal{J}$ meaning we have more than enough axioms for the justification to hold. Next the ContractAxioms subroutine removes the axioms from superset S' until only axioms that entail η remain. Finally the justification $\mathcal{J}$ is returned.

3.4.3 Expansion Algorithm ExpandAxioms($\mathcal{K}, \alpha$)

The algorithm begins by checking if entailment holds in lines 1-2. If not, the algorithm terminates and returns an empty set, else lines 3-13 are executed. Lines

4, 5, and 6 initialise a subset S with an empty set, a subset S' with an empty set and a signature Σ with the entailment's corresponding signature. Increase the set of expanded axioms by ensuring that all defining terms for the signature are present in the expansion set S. This process is repeated until $S = S'$. Thereafter, the algorithm returns a set that is a superset of $\mathcal{J}$. Figure 3.5 illustrates how the ExpandAxioms algorithm identifies axioms that are added to S until $S \models \eta$. This is denoted by the circles that have a red outline.

Algorithm 3 to compute the expansion was proposed by Horridge [26].

Algorithm 3: ExpandAxioms($\mathcal{K}, \alpha$)

Input: Knowledge base $\mathcal{K}$ Entailment η
Output: Set S

1   **if** $\mathcal{K} \not\models \eta$ **then**
2   **return** $\emptyset$
3   **else**
4       $S \quad \emptyset$
5       $S' \quad \emptyset$
6       $\Sigma \leftarrow$ signature(η)
7   **repeat**
8           $S' \quad S$
9           $S \leftarrow S \cup$ GetDefiningAxioms$(\Sigma, \mathcal{K})$
10   **if** $S \models \eta$ **then**
11   **return** S
12         $\Sigma \leftarrow$ GetSignature(S)
13   **until** $S' = S$
14 **return** S

3.4.4   Contraction Algorithm ContractAxioms($\mathcal{K}, \alpha$)

The contraction algorithm prunes the set S by removing all axioms such that if removed, $S \models \eta$ is still true. The algorithm takes in as input two sets S_{whole}, $S_{support}$ and an entailment η (where $(S_{whole} \cup S_{working}) \models \eta$). First, the base case where S_{whole} contains one axiom is checked. S_{whole} is returned if it contains one axiom and the algorithm terminates otherwise lines 3-10 are executed. In line 3 S_{whole} is split into two using the Split subroutine.

To start the pruning process, each half is first combined with a set of supporting axioms $S_{support}$ to see if they independently entail η. If one of the halves entails η, then the other half is essentially thrown away (lines 4-7). If justifications for η are spread across both halves, then each half is divided and search by a recursive call of the routine (lines 8-9) and the results are combined and returned (line 10) [26]. This is shown in Figure 3.5 by the blue circles that have a red outline only.

Algorithm 4 to compute the contraction of axioms was proposed by Horridge [26].

Algorithm 4: ContractAxioms($\mathcal{K}$, α)

   Input: Entailment η and Set S
   Output: Set S
   return ContractAxiomsRecursive($\emptyset, \mathcal{K}, \eta$)
   ContractAxiomsRecursive($S_{support}, S_{whole}, \eta$)

1 **if** $|S_{whole}| = 1$ **then**
2   **return** S_{whole}

3 S_L, S_R Split(S_{whole})
4 **if** $S_{support} \cup S_L \models \eta$ **then**
5   **return** ContractAxiomsRecursive($S_{support}, S_L, \eta$)

6 **if** $S_{support} \cup S_R \models \eta$ **then**
7   **return** ContractAxiomsRecursive($S_{support}, S_R, \eta$)

8 S_L' ContractAxiomsRecursive($S_{support} \cup S_R, S_L, \eta$)
9 S_R' ContractAxiomsRecursive($S_{support} \cup S_L', S_R, \eta$)
10 **return** $S_L' \cup S_R'$

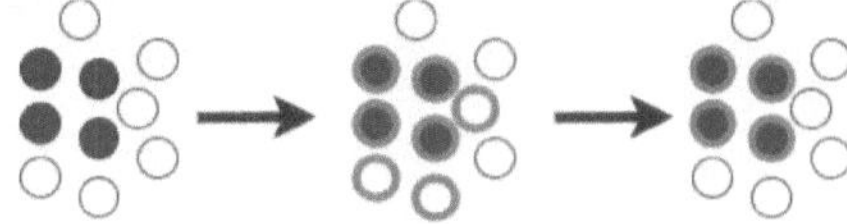

Figure 3.5: Illustration of the Expansion and Contraction Algorithms

3.5   Explanation for Entailments

The argument for extending classical reasoning services with explanations has been made clear in the sections above. Explanation facilities are useful in understanding entailments, debugging and repairing information declared in knowledge bases and also knowledge base comprehension [5, 26]. Additionally, explanation has been shown to be crucial for user acceptance and satisfaction in many studies [6]. There has been a significant amount of research devoted to the area of explanation. In particular, a specific type of explanation called justifications [26]. However, users still have trouble in understanding justifications. Thus, another research area has emerged that uses justifications as a foundation for explanations but expresses them in natural languages such as English for easy readability. It is important to mention that justifications are not the only way to express explanations but rather they are the most commonly used because they appear to be closer to the way people do reasoning, more concise and readable than reasoning-based explanations [40]. An example of a system that generates explanations in English is SWAT (Semantic Web Authoring Tool). It is an ontology editor written in java that assists users to create and modify DL knowledge bases in a controlled language called OWL Simplified English (OSE) [40, 42]. In order to generate an explanation, the editor starts by computing justifications of the entailment using the algorithms by Horridge [26] described in Section 3.4. Next, it constructs one or more proof trees for each justification. In scenarios where an entailment has multiple justifications it selects one and presents that to the users. For more information on the SWAT editor and natural language explanations the reader is directed to the paper by Tu Nguyen [40].

Translating justifications into English sentences to make them more understandable by users is beyond the scope of this **book**. However, it is important that we discuss it because the work by Tu Nguyen [40] is based on description logics, thus it can serve as a starting point to extend defeasible description logics with explanations in natural languages such as English.

3.6   Summary

In this chapter we discussed justifications. We highlighted why justifications are the most common form of explanations and also discussed the algorithms that compute them. Recall that Example 2 had two justifications that could be used to prove the entailment SpecialPenguin $\sqsubseteq$ Fly. We briefly mentioned the reason why $\mathcal{J}_2$ could not be used (because of contradictions in the knowledge base) but we shall make it more concrete in the following chapter.

The next chapter describes the issue of handling exceptions in $\mathcal{ALC}$ knowledge bases and explains in detail some of the existing approaches which address the issue.

Chapter 4

Defeasible Reasoning

In this chapter we discuss defeasible reasoning, an area dedicated to extending classical logics with non-monotonic reasoning features. Defeasible reasoning makes it possible to reason with incomplete information, specifically information that is dynamic and changes when new information is presented. Defeasible reasoning is particularly useful to represent defaults. A default is a rule that can be used unless it is overridden by an exception.

Before we continue our discussion on defeasible reasoning, let us clarify what the distinction between defeasible reasoning and non-monotonic reasoning is. A logic is said to be non-monotonic if entailed conclusions can be withdrawn by adding new information to the existing set of knowledge. For a language to be non-monotonic, it must first satisfy a set of requirements. On the other hand, defeasible logics enable us to talk about things or statements that present a typical rather than direct logical dependency. For example, the statement "birds typically fly" formally represented by $b \mathrel{|\!\sim} f$ in the propositional case talks about the fact that if something is a bird then it is reasonable to infer that it typically flies.

The idea is that non-monotonic reasoning is a form of defeasible reasoning, but there are aspects of defeasible reasoning that do not qualify as non-monotonic reasoning. For example if we look at the descriptions logics case there is some work in which quantifiers are used as a formal way in which to represent statements like α's are (typically, normally, usually) β's [1, 22, 43]. Such versions that have defeasibilty in the language are not always non-monotonic because they might not satisfy all the non-monotonic properties in specific non-monotonic reasoning systems such as the KLM approach. On the other hand For this reason we discuss defeasible reasoning because we want a language that admits the representation of typicality and can also perform defeasible entailment through defeasible subsumption which in our case also happens to be non-monotonic. This is explained in detail in Section 4.2 and Section 4.2.2.

In this **book** and chapter we focus on the extensions made for the description logics case. Section 4.1 of the chapter presents an overview of defeasible reasoning. In Section 4.2 we look at a specific approach to defeasible reasoning that has a description logic representation. Finally, we discuss the Rational Closure algorithm in Section 4.3 which is the method we shall use to compute entailments that contain defeasible information.

4.1   Overview

Reasoning with exceptions has been a major topic in AI since the 80s [15]. Classical monotonic formalisms such as description logics, are not adequate to properly represent and perform reasoning on defeasible information. This is because the monotonicity property of most classic formalisms specifies that adding any explicit information to a knowledge base should never remove an inference entailed by the knowledge base without said information [39]. In other words, classical formalisms assume that the information defined in knowledge bases is error-free and does not allow exceptions [15].

Example 3 Consider a monotonic system that contains the following information in its knowledge base: "Birds usually fly and penguins are birds". The reasoner will conclude that penguins usually fly. Assuming new information "penguins do not fly" is added to the knowledge base, the reasoner will still conclude that penguins usually fly. However, we know from the new information that penguins do not fly, thus creating a conflict (penguins that usually fly and penguins that do not fly) which results in the fact that there are no penguins.

In order to accommodate cases that will require retraction of entailed conclusions defeasible reasoning is concerned with coming up with frameworks and algorithms that allows the representation and manipulation about defeasible statements. Generally we want a framework in which it is dealt with in the way we as humans do. A statement is defeasible when the information it presents does not highlight a strict relationship, and any conclusion drawn from the statement is contextual rather than definitive [31]. Let us consider the following bird example.

Example 4 Suppose a non-monotonic system contains the following information in its knowledge base: birds typically fly, birds typically have wings and penguins are birds. When queried with the statement "do penguins typically fly?", it should respond "Yes, penguins typically fly". Now suppose more information is added to our knowledge base such that our new knowledge base contains: birds typically fly, birds typically have wings, penguins are birds and penguins do not fly. When queried the same statement "do penguins typically fly?", the reasoner should respond and say "No, penguins do not fly".

Using the same knowledge base that contains the statements: birds typically fly, birds typically have wings and penguins are birds. When queried "do penguins have wings?", the answer is going to be "Yes". Just like before if new information is added to the knowledge base such that our new knowledge base contains: birds typically fly, birds typically have wings, penguins are birds and penguins do not fly. When the system is queried the same question "do penguins have wings?", the reasoner should respond and say "No". However if we ask the reasoner "do penguins not have wings", the reasoner will respond "No".

What this example generally shows is that there are two distinct issues when we query a knowledge base and the reasoner gives an answer "No". Sometimes the answer is no because we can not deduce from our knowledge base that an entailment holds e.g. "do penguins not have wings" and sometimes the no is because we have been explicitly told in the knowledge base e.g. that "penguins do not fly".

From Example 3, the entailed conclusions are considered as part of the information within the knowledge base whereas in Example 4 the entailed conclusions can be retracted because they are separate from information explicitly stated in the knowledge base. In other words, Example 4 illustrates that if the addition of new information to the knowledge base in a non-monotonic system causes inconsistencies we can retract conclusions that were made earlier.

The general principle of non-monotonic reasoning is that certain statements are retracted. The approach we take is such that we draw the distinction between those statements that are explicitly mentioned and those that are derived. Additionally, we never retract (override) the explicit statements but we can retract the derived statements.

As a result various approaches to non-monotonic reasoning in KR formalisms have been developed which include: Default Logic [44], Circumscription [36], Probabilistic logic [41] and Preferential approaches [12].

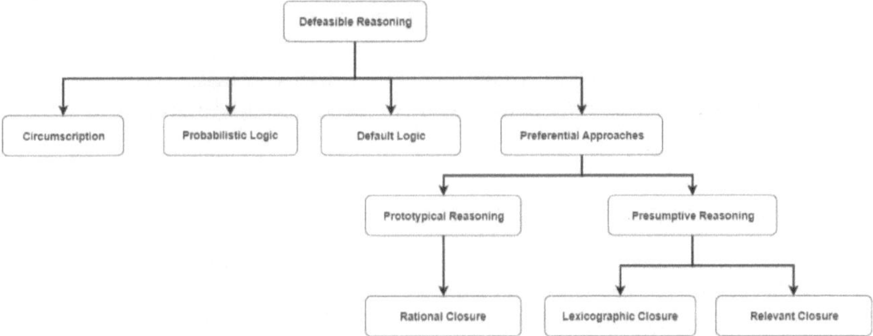

Figure 4.1: Various approaches to Defeasible Reasoning

Figure 4.1 shows the different approaches to defeasible reasoning and also illustrates the two main strategies within the preferential approaches and their specific methods. It is important to note that Figure 4.1 is not the complete representation of the entire defeasible reasoning field but rather it gives a tree structure to show the different approaches and how they are categorised and where this book fits in. Recall that the underlying Knowledge Representation formalism for this book is description logics. This means our focus is on those approaches that have a description logics representation, specifically $\mathcal{ALC}$. Although there have been many proposals to extend description logics with non-monotonic features, identifying a defeasible description logic that is adequate enough in terms of expressivity and computational complexity is a non-trivial task. The literature shows that there is existing work for extending description logics with defeasible reasoning for Circumscription [7], Probabilistic Logic [8], Negation as Failure [30] and Preferential reasoning approaches [12, 15, 37, 39]. However, we shall not go into detail of each but rather drill down one specific approach and that is the preferential approach to non-monotonic reasoning. The motivation for focusing on the preferential approach is that preferential extensions of description logics are based on work that has been well studied in the propositional case by Kraus, Lehmann and Magidor [32, 34] and is often referred to as the *KLM approach* [13, 12, 15, 39, 49]. The KLM approach has a formal definition of defeasible entailment. What this means is that we have a logic with a form of entailment that is different from classical logic. Although it is an extension of classical logic, it turns out that the KLM approach has the ability to compute defeasible entailment. Computation of defeasible entailment can be done by simply reducing it to classical entailment which is a solved problem. In other words, the important part is that there is a formal definition of defeasible entailment and one of the computational advantages is that it can be reduced to classical entailment [17]. Additionally an implementation of this approach is available for the ontology editor Protégé [17, 39].

In the following section, we first look at what preferential descriptions logics are and give a summary of important definitions that are required to understand how we generate explanations. Then we conclude the chapter by discussing the Rational Closure algorithm which is the specific method we have selected to perform defeasible entailment.

4.2   Preferential Description Logics

In this section, we first look at a non-monotonic extension made for propositional logic and then present the foundations of the preferential approach to defeasible reasoning in description logics.

4.2.1   Overview of Preferential Propositional Logics

In the 1990 KLM paper [32] the defeasible implication operator ($\mathrel{|\!\sim}$) was thought of as a replacement for classical entailment ($\models$). What this meant is that a classical propositional statement α and a classical propositional statement β and the $\mathrel{|\!\sim}$ is thought of as a defeasible entailment operator on classical propositional logics. So it is another form of entailment. However the underlying language is still classical logics. Therefore, the properties in the original paper include rules such as:

$\alpha \mathrel{|\!\sim} \alpha$	To represent Reflexivity which means it is typically the case that α follows from α
$\dfrac{\alpha \mathrel{|\!\sim} \beta,\ \alpha \wedge \beta \mathrel{|\!\sim} \gamma}{\alpha \mathrel{|\!\sim} \gamma}$	For Cumulative Transitivity which is interpreted as if α typically implies β and assume further that α and β typically implies γ then we would expect that α typically implies γ

Table 4.1: Some of the Properties for Preferential Propositional Logics [35]

However, later on Lehmann and Magidor [34] interpreted ($\mathrel{|\!\sim}$) differently from a defeasible consequence relation to logical connective such as $\neg, \wedge, \vee, \rightarrow$ and $\leftrightarrow$. This is because previously we could not write down statements such as "most typical α's are β's " because $\mathrel{|\!\sim}$ was a consequence relation. With the shift from $\mathrel{|\!\sim}$ being a consequence relation to a connective we can now use it in our language to describe defeasible statements. However, note that $\mathrel{|\!\sim}$ is different from the other logical connectives because you can not nest $\mathrel{|\!\sim}$ and have statements such as $\alpha \mathrel{|\!\sim} \beta \mathrel{|\!\sim} \gamma$. Nesting $\mathrel{|\!\sim}$ means the language becomes more expressive and most of the technical results will not hold in the new language.

The result was an enriched language with an operator that enables writing down of defeasible implication statements also referred to in the literature as conditional assertions written as $\alpha \mathrel{|\!\sim} \beta$, where α and β are propositional formulas [39]. The meaning attached to such an assertion is as follows: if α represents the information I have about the true state of the world, I will jump to the conclusion that β is true [34]. In other words "typically or normally α entails β". For example, the statement that "birds normally fly" will be represented by the conditional assertion $\mathsf{b} \mathrel{|\!\sim} \mathsf{f}$, where b and f are propositional variables representing being a bird and flying respectively.

The advantages of enriching propositional logics with the preferential approach to defeasible reasoning is that compared to other non-monotonic methods, the system's computational complexity is not blown up with respect to the classical case and defeasible entailment can be reduced to classical entailment checking. A related point of interest is that it has a well-known connection with Belief Revision [16]. Belief revision consists of incorporating a new belief, changing as few as possible of the original beliefs while preserving consistency upon having access to new information [23, 24].

This means now that we have a richer language, a new representation and definition is required to denote defeasible entailment. The symbol $\mathrel{\approx\!\!\!|}$ is analogous to the role that classical entailment $\models$ plays in classical description logics and we shall define how to interpret defeasible entailment in Section 4.3.

4.2.2   Preferential Description Logics

The adoption of the preferential extensions of description logics is due to the following reasons: first of all, the preferential approach has been well studied for the propositional case and it provides an in-depth analysis of the properties that any non-monotonic consequence relation should satisfy. Thus, it is reasonable to expect that most of the aforementioned features and advantages of the KLM approach for the propositional case discussed in Section 4.2.1 should transfer to KLM-based extensions of description logics, as well.

In Section 4.2.1 we discussed how initially $\mathrel{|\!\sim}$ was taken as an alternative to the classical entailment relation $\models$ but Lehmann and Magidor [32] changed its interpretation to a connective and that there is a different defeasible entailment relation $\mathrel{\approx\!\!\!|}$ which is separate from $\models$.

Now we are moving the same translation to description logics. Consider $\rightarrow$ which is material implication in classical propositional logics, the description logics analog would be the subsumption operator $\sqsubseteq$. This is because if we were to write the statement "birds fly" in propositional logics we would write $\mathsf{Bird} \rightarrow \mathsf{Fly}$ and in the description logics case $\mathsf{Bird} \sqsubseteq \mathsf{Fly}$. So the analog is that we are going from the implication operator $\rightarrow$ to the subsumption operator $\sqsubseteq$.

Propositional Logics	Description Logics
$\mathsf{Bird} \rightarrow \mathsf{Fly}$	$\mathsf{Bird} \sqsubseteq \mathsf{Fly}$
$\mathsf{Bird} \mathrel{|\!\sim} \mathsf{Fly}$	$\mathsf{Bird} \mathrel{\sqsubset\!\!\!\sim} \mathsf{Fly}$

Table 4.2: Classical and defeasible equivalences between propositional logics and description logics

Therefore, if in the propositional case we have a 'defeasible arrow' which is $\mathrel{\vert\!\sim}$, then the defeasible subsumption will be $\mathrel{\sqsubseteq\!\sim}$ for description logics. Now we can correctly represent the statement "birds typically fly" as $\text{Bird} \mathrel{\vert\!\sim} \text{Fly}$ and $\text{Bird} \mathrel{\sqsubseteq\!\sim} \text{Fly}$ for the propositional and description logics case respectively.

In general, preferential description logics enrich the classical description logics with the *defeasible subsumption relation* $\mathrel{\sqsubseteq\!\sim}$. In this **book** we focus on $\mathcal{ALC}$, however there are more expressive description logics that have defeasible definitions. The statement $C \mathrel{\sqsubseteq\!\sim} D$ is a defeasible subsumption statement which means that the most *typical* C's are D's as opposed to all C's being D's in the classical case. We now present the necessary definitions required to complete the description of preferential description logics adopted from Britz et al. [12].

Definition 8 (Defeasible Concept Inclusion) Let $C, D \in \mathcal{L}$. A defeasible concept inclusion axiom *(DCI, for short)* is a statement of the form $C \mathrel{\sqsubseteq\!\sim} D$. A defeasible concept inclusion of the form $C \mathrel{\sqsubseteq\!\sim} D$ is to be read as *"usually, an instance of the class C is also an instance of the class D"*.

For example, the DCI:

$$\text{Bird} \mathrel{\sqsubseteq\!\sim} \text{Fly}$$

will be read as "Birds usually Fly". Intuitively, the semantics for $\mathrel{\sqsubseteq\!\sim}$ states that given a defeasible subsumption axiom $C \mathrel{\sqsubseteq\!\sim} D$ (where C and D may be complex $\mathcal{ALC}$ descriptions), then this statement means that all typical C's are also D's (as opposed to all C's being D's in the classical case). Furthermore, it is worth noting that $\mathrel{\sqsubseteq\!\sim}$, just as $\sqsubseteq$, is a 'connective' sitting between the concept language (object level) and the metalanguage (that of entailment) and it is meant to be the defeasible counterpart of the classical subsumption $\sqsubseteq$ [12].

Definition 9 (Defeasible TBox) A defeasible TBox (*DTBox, for short*) is a finite set of DCIs. Given a TBox $\mathcal{T}$ and a DTBox $\mathcal{D}$, we let $\mathcal{K} := \mathcal{T} \cup \mathcal{D}$ and refer to it as a defeasible knowledge base.

Example 5 The following defeasible knowledge base gives a formal specification for our bird scenario:

$$\mathcal{T} = \left\{ \begin{array}{l} \text{Penguin} \sqsubseteq \text{Bird,} \\ \text{Robin} \sqsubseteq \text{Bird} \end{array} \right\}$$

$$\mathcal{D} = \left\{ \begin{array}{l} \text{Bird} \mathrel{\sqsubseteq\!\sim} \text{Fly,} \\ \text{Bird} \mathrel{\sqsubseteq\!\sim} \text{Wings,} \\ \text{Penguin} \mathrel{\sqsubseteq\!\sim} \neg\text{Fly} \end{array} \right\}$$

Now that we have the language with a defeasible subsumption it tells us that whenever we write down the defeasible entailment symbol $\mathrel{\vert\!\approx}$, there is not only one form of defeasible entailment but we place constraints on what is allowed by looking at the six properties below.

Definition 10 (Defeasible Entailment Relation) A defeasible entailment relation $\mathrel{\vert\!\approx}$ is preferential if it satisfies the following set of properties, which are referred to as (the description logics versions of the) preferential KLM properties.

$$(REF) \quad \mathcal{K} \mathrel{\vert\!\approx} C \mathrel{\sqsubset\!\sim} C \quad \text{Reflexivity}$$

$$(AND) \quad \frac{\mathcal{K} \mathrel{\vert\!\approx} C \mathrel{\sqsubset\!\sim} D, \ \mathcal{K} \mathrel{\vert\!\approx} C \mathrel{\sqsubset\!\sim} E}{\mathcal{K} \mathrel{\vert\!\approx} C \sqcap D \mathrel{\sqsubset\!\sim} E}$$

$$(CM) \quad \frac{\mathcal{K} \mathrel{\vert\!\approx} C \mathrel{\sqsubset\!\sim} D, \ \mathcal{K} \mathrel{\vert\!\approx} C \mathrel{\sqsubset\!\sim} E}{\mathcal{K} \mathrel{\vert\!\approx} C \sqcap D \mathrel{\sqsubset\!\sim} E} \quad \text{Cautious Monotony}$$

$$(LLE) \quad \frac{\mathcal{K} \mathrel{\vert\!\approx} C \equiv D, \ \mathcal{K} \mathrel{\vert\!\approx} C \mathrel{\sqsubset\!\sim} E}{\mathcal{K} \mathrel{\vert\!\approx} D \mathrel{\sqsubset\!\sim} E} \quad \text{Left Logical Equivalence}$$

$$(RW) \quad \frac{\mathcal{K} \mathrel{\vert\!\approx} C \mathrel{\sqsubset\!\sim} D, \ \mathcal{K} \mathrel{\vert\!\approx} D \sqsubseteq E}{\mathcal{K} \mathrel{\vert\!\approx} C \mathrel{\sqsubset\!\sim} E} \quad \text{Right Weakening}$$

$$(OR) \quad \frac{\mathcal{K} \mathrel{\vert\!\approx} C \mathrel{\sqsubset\!\sim} E, \ \mathcal{K} \mathrel{\vert\!\approx} D \mathrel{\sqsubset\!\sim} E}{\mathcal{K} \mathrel{\vert\!\approx} C \sqcup D \mathrel{\sqsubset\!\sim} E} \quad \text{Left Disjunction}$$

These are generally considered as the core properties defining and satisfying defeasible entailment [18]. Recall that the defeasible subsumption $\mathrel{\sqsubset\!\sim}$ is an operator in our defeasible $\mathcal{ALC}$ language. Therefore, if we look at the properties they state how the defeasible operator $\mathrel{\vert\!\approx}$ and defeasible subsumption $\mathrel{\sqsubset\!\sim}$ should behave. For example if we take Cautious Monotony,

$$(CM) \quad \frac{\mathcal{K} \mathrel{\vert\!\approx} C \mathrel{\sqsubset\!\sim} D, \ \mathcal{K} \mathrel{\vert\!\approx} C \mathrel{\sqsubset\!\sim} E}{\mathcal{K} \mathrel{\vert\!\approx} C \sqcap D \mathrel{\sqsubset\!\sim} E} \quad \text{Cautious Monotony}$$

it states that if C is usually included in D and we know that C is usually included in E, then you can strengthen the left hand side by combining C and D using a conjunction $\sqcap$ without bring back full monotonicity. This means that the antecedent is strengthened in a controlled way because it is only done by adding something (D) that is related to C.

If we look at the properties from Reflexivity to Left Disjunction i.e., all the preferential entailment relations, they form a broad class of defeasible entailment relations. These properties place constraints on what defeasible entailment allows. However, when we look at the properties some do not satisfy rational monotonicity. In order to restrict the class of defeasible entailment relations we can add rational monotonicity to the preferential entailment relations to obtain one of the many classes of defeasible entailment relations. This results into rational closure which is our main focus and one possible class from the broad class of defeasible entailment relations.

$$(RM) \quad \frac{\mathcal{K} \mathrel{\vert\!\approx} C \mathrel{\sqsubset\!\sim} E, \ \mathcal{K} \mathrel{\vert\!\not\approx} C \mathrel{\sqsubset\!\sim} \neg D}{C \sqcap D \mathrel{\sqsubset\!\sim} E} \quad \text{Rational Monotony}$$

(RM) is generally considered as the strongest form of monotonicity we can use in the characterisation of a reasoning system in order to formalise a well-behaved form of defeasible reasoning [19]. Semantically, rational defeasible entailment relations can be characterised by means of a particular kind of possible-worlds structure that is, ranked interpretations [18]. In this **book** we will not discuss the semantics because it is beyond the scope of this **book** but the reader is referred to Britz et al. [13] for more details.

Note that we have presented the preferential defeasible entailment relations first because this is how they were formulated first and also how they are usually presented in the literature. However, we are only interested in the algorithmic description of rational closure which looks at the ranking of statements based on their exceptionality and is one class of the many classes of defeasible entailment relations.

4.3   Rational Closure

The rational closure algorithm allows us to perform one form of rational entailment over defeasible knowledge bases and in order to do that every statement in the defeasible knowledge base in question should be assigned a ranking. The algorithm to compute rational closure is summarised as follows: the rational closure algorithm works by ranking defeasible statements. Once the defeasible statements have been ranked, they are then treated as classical statements. In order to rank the defeasible statements the rational closure algorithm uses a notion referred to as exceptionality. Intuitively, exceptionality arranges statements in the knowledge base according to specificity because we are trying to determine how general or specific statements are. The statements that are considered as more general than others (defeasible statements) will be discarded first (if necessary) and the specific statements (classical statements) will be discarded last. In order to determine if a statement is exceptional or not, a materialisation of defeasible statements needs to be performed. Materialisation allows us to rewrite a defeasible statement such as $C \mathbin{\sqsubseteq\mkern-10mu\sim} D$ to its classical analog $C \sqsubseteq D$. Figure 4.2 shows the steps required to compute rational closure.

Generally, if we have both classical and defeasible statements in our defeasible knowledge base, the way in which we want to rank the statements is that all the statements that are classical need to have a rank of infinite (∞) because generally they are not going to be discarded.

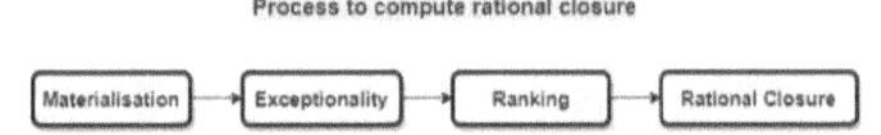

Figure 4.2: Process to computer rational closure

The definition of materialisation is presented first because it is needed to define exceptionality.

Definition 11 (Materialisation). Let $\mathcal{D}$ be a set of DCIs. With $\overline{\mathcal{D}} =_{def} \{\neg C \sqcup D \mid C \mathbin{\sqsubseteq\mkern-10mu\sim} D \in \mathcal{D}\}$ we denote the materialisation of $\mathcal{D}$.

- $\overline{\mathcal{K}}$ contains the TBox $\mathcal{T}$ and the materialization of the DTBox $\mathcal{D}$ such that $\overline{\mathcal{K}} = \mathcal{T} \cup \overline{\mathcal{D}}$

As you can see from the definition the materialisation of a defeasible statement $C \mathbin{\sqsubseteq\mkern-10mu\sim} D$ is $\top \sqsubseteq \neg C \sqcup D$

Materialisation allows us to rewrite a defeasible statement such as $C \mathbin{\sqsubseteq\mkern-10mu\sim} D$ to its classical analog $C \sqsubseteq D$ which can be further rewritten as $\top \sqsubseteq \neg C \sqcup D$ so that we can use the classical version for entailment checking. We shall expand this point shortly.

Definition 12 (Exceptionality). Let $\mathcal{K}$ be a defeasible knowledge base and $C \in \mathcal{L}$.

- C is exceptional w.r.t. $\mathcal{K}$ iff $\overline{\mathcal{K}} \models C \sqsubseteq \bot$

- $C \mathrel{\vrule height 1.3ex depth 0pt\joinrel\sim} D$ is exceptional w.r.t. $\mathcal{K}$ iff C is exceptional w.r.t. $\mathcal{K}$

The Exceptional function used to compute exceptionality of statements was proposed by Britz et al. [11]

Function Exceptional$(\mathcal{T}, \mathcal{D}')$

Input: $\mathcal{T}$ and $\mathcal{D}' \subseteq \mathcal{D}$
Output: $\mathcal{E} \subseteq \mathcal{D}'$ such that $\mathcal{E}$ is exceptional w.r.t. $\mathcal{T} \cup \mathcal{D}'$
1 $\mathcal{E} \leftarrow \emptyset$
2 **foreach** $C \mathrel{\vrule height 1.3ex depth 0pt\joinrel\sim} D \in \mathcal{D}'$ **do**
3   **if** $\mathcal{T} \models \bigsqcap \overline{\mathcal{D}} \sqsubseteq \neg C$ **then**
4       $\mathcal{E} \leftarrow \mathcal{E} \cup \{C \mathrel{\vrule height 1.3ex depth 0pt\joinrel\sim} D\}$
5 **return** $\mathcal{E}$

Thus, our interest is to rank the defeasible statements because they might have a finite or infinite rank. In other words any classical statement in the original defeasible knowledge base must be exceptional therefore should have a rank of infinite.

Finally the ranked statements are used in the main algorithm to determine whether or not the query is entailed from the defeasible knowledge base.

Let us expand on the notion of materialisation. Looking at line 3 in the Exceptional function, the TBox $\mathcal{T}$ is on the LHS of $\models$ which is entailment and we place the DTBox statements on the LHS of the subsumption relation $\sqsubseteq$ and place the concept we want to check for on the RHS of $\sqsubseteq$ in this case $\neg C$. Intuitively, suppose we have a TBox $\mathcal{T}$ and a DTBox $\mathcal{D}$ with a number of defeasible subsumption statements $(C_1 \mathrel{\vrule height 1.1ex depth 0pt\joinrel\sim} D_1), (C_2 \mathrel{\vrule height 1.1ex depth 0pt\joinrel\sim} D_2), \ldots (C_n \mathrel{\vrule height 1.1ex depth 0pt\joinrel\sim} D_n)$. In order to check for exceptionality, the TBox statements do not change and are kept on the LHS of the entailment relation $\models$. Then the DTBox statements are turned into concepts $(\neg C_1 \sqcup D_1), (\neg C_2 \sqcup D_2), \ldots, (\neg C_n \sqcup D_n)$ but in order for the concepts to hold at the same time they need to be combined using a conjunction $\sqcap$ thus the final statement is $(\neg C_1 \sqcup D_1) \sqcap (\neg C_2 \sqcup D_2) \sqcap \ldots \sqcap (\neg C_n \sqcup D_n)$ which is the conjunction of concepts which refers to the defeasible subsumption statements.

So the definition of materialisation says, if you have a defeasible DTBox $\mathcal{D}$ rewrite each statement to its concept analog as shown in Definition 11 and then combine all of them using a conjunction.

To determine the exceptionality of statements, Exceptional uses of the notion of materialisation to reduce concept exceptionality checking to entailment checking. Exceptionality refers to information in which there are exceptions to stated rules. Essentially, the Exceptional function is arranging the statements in a knowledge base according to specificity because we are trying to determine how general or specific statements are. To use the classic example, a bird has wings and flies, and a penguin is a bird that does not fly. Therefore, a penguin is an *exceptional* bird. More precisely, if line 3 in the **Exceptional** function holds add the defeasible statement to $\mathcal{E}$.

Now that we have defined materialisation and exceptionality we can illustrate the computation of ranking using the following example.

Example 6 Let $\mathcal{K} = \mathcal{T} \cup \mathcal{D}$ be a defeasible knowledge base. The first step of the algorithm is to assign a rank to each defeasible concept inclusion (DCI) in $\mathcal{D}$ by determining their exceptionality.

$$\mathcal{T} = \left\{ \begin{array}{c} \mathsf{Penguin} \sqsubseteq \mathsf{Bird},\\ \mathsf{Robin} \sqsubseteq \mathsf{Bird} \end{array} \right\} \text{ and let } \mathcal{D} = \left\{ \begin{array}{c} \mathsf{Bird} \mathrel{\sqsubset\!\!\!\sim} \mathsf{Fly},\\ \mathsf{Bird} \mathrel{\sqsubset\!\!\!\sim} \mathsf{Wings},\\ \mathsf{Penguin} \mathrel{\sqsubset\!\!\!\sim} \neg\mathsf{Fly} \end{array} \right\}$$

The **ComputeRanking** function used to compute ranking of statements was proposed by Britz et al. [11]

Function ComputeRanking($\mathcal{K}$)

    Input: $\mathcal{K} = \mathcal{T} \cup \mathcal{D}$
    Output: $\mathcal{K}^* = \mathcal{T}^* \cup \mathcal{D}^*$, an exceptionality sequence $\mathcal{E}_0, \dots, \mathcal{E}_n$ and a
                  partitioning $R = \{\mathcal{D}_0, \dots, \mathcal{D}_n\}$ for $\mathcal{D}^*$

1 $\mathcal{T}^* \leftarrow \mathcal{T}$
2 $\mathcal{D}^* \leftarrow \mathcal{D}$
3 $R \leftarrow \emptyset$
4 **repeat**
5     $i \leftarrow 0$
6     $\mathcal{E}_0 \leftarrow \mathcal{D}^*$
7     $\mathcal{E}_1 \leftarrow \text{Exceptional}(\mathcal{T}^*, \mathcal{E}_0)$
8     $\mathcal{E}_{sequence} \leftarrow \mathcal{E}_0 \cup \mathcal{E}_1$
9   **while** $\mathcal{E}_{i+1} \neq \mathcal{E}_i$ **do**
10        $i \leftarrow i + 1$
11        $\mathcal{E}_{i+1} \leftarrow \text{Exceptional}(\mathcal{T}^*, \mathcal{E}_i)$
12        $\mathcal{E}_{sequence} \leftarrow \mathcal{E}_{sequence} \cup \{\mathcal{E}_{i+1}\}$
13     $\mathcal{D}^*_\infty \leftarrow \mathcal{E}_i$
14     $\mathcal{T}^* \leftarrow \mathcal{T}^* \cup \{C \sqsubseteq D \mid C \mathrel{\sqsubset\!\!\!\sim} D \in \mathcal{D}^*_\infty\}$
15     $\mathcal{D}^* \leftarrow \mathcal{D}^* \setminus \mathcal{D}^*_\infty$
16 **until** $\mathcal{D}^*_\infty = \emptyset$
17 **for** $j \leftarrow 1$ *to* i **do**
18     $\mathcal{D}_{j-1} \leftarrow \mathcal{E}_{j-1} \setminus \mathcal{E}_j$
19     $R \leftarrow R \cup \{\mathcal{D}_{j-1}\}$
20 **return** $\mathcal{K}^* = \mathcal{T}^* \cup \mathcal{D}^*, \mathcal{E}_{sequence}, R$

Using the defeasible knowledge base in example 6, **ComputeRanking** will be executed as follows.

1. The **ComputeRanking** function receives a knowledge base $\mathcal{K} = \mathcal{T} \cup \mathcal{D}$ and returns a knowledge base $\mathcal{K}^* = \mathcal{T}^* \cup \mathcal{D}^*$, an exceptionality sequence $\mathcal{E}_0, \dots, \mathcal{E}_n$ and a ranking R which is a collection of sets of sentences. Lines 1, 2 and 3 initialise $\mathcal{T}^*$ to $\mathcal{T}$, $\mathcal{D}^*$ to $\mathcal{D}$ and R to an empty set respectively.

2. The next section of the ComputeRanking function from lines 4-15 uses the Exceptional function to determine exceptionality of each DCI in D. We first set a counter i to 0 in line 5 and then assign the first set of exceptional statements $\mathcal{E}_0$ to $\mathcal{D}$ which in our case is the original DTBox $\mathcal{D}$ in line 6.

$$\mathcal{E}_0 = \{\text{Bird} \mathrel{\sqsubset\!\!\sim} \text{Fly}, \text{Bird} \mathrel{\sqsubset\!\!\sim} \text{Wings}, \text{Penguin} \mathrel{\sqsubset\!\!\sim} \neg\text{Fly}\}$$

3. We make the first call to Exceptional and assign the output to $\mathcal{E}_1$. We briefly switch to the definition of the Exceptional function.

4. The Exceptional function receives a TBox $\mathcal{T}$ and DTBox $\mathcal{D}$ as input and returns a set $\mathcal{E}$ which is a subset of $\mathcal{D}$ such that $\mathcal{E}$ is exceptional w.r.t. $\mathcal{T} \cup \mathcal{D}$.

   (i) We start by initialising $\mathcal{E}$ to the empty set in line 1.

   (ii) Then in lines 2-4 we check every defeasible statement in $\mathcal{D}$ to see if the materialisation entails $\neg C$. If it does we add the defeasible statement to $\mathcal{E}$ because it is exceptional (line 4).

   (iii) This process is repeated until all the statements in $\mathcal{D}$ are checked. Then the set $\mathcal{E}$ is returned in line 5.

   (iv) The for loop using Example 6 on lines 2-4 will execute as follows. We loop through each element in $\mathcal{D}$ and check if the negation of the antecedent is holds. For example the following checks if the concept Bird is exceptional:
   $$\mathcal{T} \models (\neg\text{Bird} \sqcup \text{Fly}) \sqcap (\neg\text{Bird} \sqcup \text{Wings}) \sqcap (\neg\text{Penguin} \sqcup \neg\text{Fly}) \sqsubseteq \neg\text{Bird}$$

   Whereas the following checks if the concept Penguin is exceptional:
   $$\mathcal{T} \models (\neg\text{Bird} \sqcup \text{Fly}) \sqcap (\neg\text{Bird} \sqcup \text{Wings}) \sqcap (\neg\text{Penguin} \sqcup \neg\text{Fly}) \sqsubseteq \neg\text{Penguin}$$

   (v) Going through all the statements we find that the antecedent of $\text{Penguin}\mathrel{\sqsubset\!\!\sim}\neg\text{Fly}$ in other words Penguin is exceptional and therefore because Penguin is exceptional the statement $\text{Penguin} \mathrel{\sqsubset\!\!\sim} \neg\text{Fly}$ is also exceptional by definition. Therefore the statement is added to $\mathcal{E}$ in line 4 and returned as the only exceptional statement.
   $$\mathcal{E} = \{\text{Penguin} \mathrel{\sqsubset\!\!\sim} \neg\text{Fly}\}$$

5. We now continue the description of the ComputeRanking function. After we called Exceptional in line 7 of the ComputeRanking function we then obtain the following exceptionality sequence:

$$\mathcal{E}_0 = \{\text{Bird} \mathrel{\sqsubset\!\!\sim} \text{Fly}, \text{Bird} \mathrel{\sqsubset\!\!\sim} \text{Wings}, \text{Penguin} \mathrel{\sqsubset\!\!\sim} \neg\text{Fly}\}$$

$$\mathcal{E}_1 = \{\text{Penguin} \mathrel{\sqsubset\!\!\sim} \neg\text{Fly}\}$$

Next $\mathcal{E}_0$ and $\mathcal{E}_1$ are added to $\mathcal{E}_{sequence}$ on line 8. $\mathcal{E}_{sequence}$ is used as input for the RationalClosure algorithm.

6. If $\mathcal{E}_0 \neq \mathcal{E}_1$, then we call Exceptional for $\mathcal{T}^* \cup \mathcal{E}_1$, defining the set $\mathcal{E}_2$, and so on. $\mathcal{E}_2 = \emptyset$ thus the while loop will terminate.

7. The next section of ComputeRanking lines 13-15 handle the scenario where some statements are always exceptional and are also defeasible but really need to have a rank of infinite. If this is the case the classical translation of these

defeasible statements is moved to the TBox $\mathcal{T}^*$ in line 14 and also removed from $\mathcal{D}^*$.

8. Once we have obtained the knowledge base $\mathcal{K}^* = \mathcal{T}^* \cup \mathcal{D}^*$ and the exceptionality sequence $\mathcal{E}_0, \mathcal{E}_1, \ldots, \mathcal{E}_i$ the final section of the algorithm partitions the set $\mathcal{D}^*$ into the sets $\mathcal{D}_0, \mathcal{D}_1, \ldots, \mathcal{D}_i$ for some $n \geq 0$ (Lines 17–19 of ComputeRanking). Using Example 6 the ranking is computed as follows:

$\mathcal{D}_0 = \mathcal{E}_0 \setminus \mathcal{E}_1 = \mathsf{Bird} \sqsubset\!\!\sim \mathsf{Fly}, \mathsf{Bird} \sqsubset\!\!\sim \mathsf{Wings}$

$\mathcal{D}_1 = \mathcal{E}_1 \setminus \mathcal{E}_2 = \mathsf{Penguin} \sqsubset\!\!\sim \neg\mathsf{Fly}.$

Note that defeasible statements may also have a rank of infinite (∞) for example if we have a DTBox $\mathcal{D} = \{B \sqsubset\!\!\sim A, B \sqsubset\!\!\sim \neg A\}$, both statements are exceptional and will be assigned a rank of infinite. The details of how it is possible to have defeasible statements with a rank of infinite can be deduced using the Exceptional function.

Given the knowledge base $\mathcal{K}^* = \mathcal{T}^* \cup \mathcal{D}^*$ and the exceptionality sequence $\mathcal{E}_0, \mathcal{E}_1, \ldots, \mathcal{E}_i$, we can now define the main algorithm for deciding whether a query such $C \sqsubset\!\!\sim D$ is in the rational closure of $\mathcal{K}$. Just like we did with the Exceptional function, we use the same approach of materialisations where $\overline{\mathcal{E}}_i$ the classical analog of the defeasible statements in $\mathcal{E}_i$ that is $\overline{\mathcal{E}}_i = (\neg C_1 \sqcup D_1) \sqcap (\neg C_2 \sqcup D_2) \sqcap \ldots \sqcap (\neg C_n \sqcup D_n)$.

The RationalClosure function used to compute the rational closure of statements was proposed by Britz et al. [11]

Function RationalClosure($\mathcal{K}$, α)

    Input: $\mathcal{K} = \mathcal{T} \cup \mathcal{D}$, the corresponding $\mathcal{K}^* = \mathcal{T}^* \cup \mathcal{D}^*$, the sequence $\mathcal{E}_0, \ldots, \mathcal{E}_n$, and a query $\alpha = C \sqsubset\!\!\sim D$.

    Output: `true` if $\mathcal{K} \vdash_{\mathsf{rat}} C \sqsubset\!\!\sim D$, `false` otherwise

1   $i \leftarrow 0$

2   **while** $\mathcal{T}^* \models \bigsqcap \overline{\mathcal{E}}_i \sqcap C \sqsubseteq \bot$ *and* $i \leq n$ **do**

3     $\lfloor$ $i \quad i+1$

4   **if** $i \leq n$ **then**

5     $\lfloor$ **return** $\mathcal{T}^* \models \bigsqcap \overline{\mathcal{E}}_i \sqcap C \sqsubseteq D$

6   **else**

7     $\lfloor$ **return** $\mathcal{T}^* \models C \sqsubseteq D$

The first step is to compute the ranking and exceptionality of statements. Table 4.3 shows an example of an exceptionality sequence that is used as input for the rational closure algorithm. $\mathcal{E}_0, \mathcal{E}_1, \ldots, \mathcal{E}_n$ represent all defeasible statement in order of ranking and ∞ represents all classical statements as well as those defeasible statements that are actually classical.

As the algorithm executes it checks whether the antecedent of the query results into any conflicts in the knowledge bases; i.e., $\mathcal{T}^* \models \bigsqcap \overline{\mathcal{E}}_i \sqcap C \sqsubseteq \bot$ line 2 in the RationalClosure algorithm. If the statement evaluates to true, the statements in that sequence are "thrown away" or "discarded" and the next sequence is checked.

Using the exceptionality sequence above, the rational closure algorithm in some cases returns an answer `true` and in some cases it returns `false` by "throwing" away statements at specific exceptionality levels. In some cases it does not "throw away"

$\mathcal{E}_0$	$\alpha_0 \mathbin{\sqsubseteq\!\sim} \beta_0,\ \alpha_1 \mathbin{\sqsubseteq\!\sim} \beta_1,\ \alpha_2 \mathbin{\sqsubseteq\!\sim} \beta_2$
$\mathcal{E}_1$	$\alpha_3 \mathbin{\sqsubseteq\!\sim} \beta_3,\alpha_4 \mathbin{\sqsubseteq\!\sim} \beta_4$
$\mathcal{E}_2$	$\alpha_5 \mathbin{\sqsubseteq\!\sim} \beta_5$
$\vdots$	$\alpha_6 \mathbin{\sqsubseteq\!\sim} \beta_6,\ \alpha_7 \mathbin{\sqsubseteq\!\sim} \beta_7$
$\mathcal{E}_n$	$\alpha_8 \mathbin{\sqsubseteq\!\sim} \beta_8,\ \alpha_9 \mathbin{\sqsubseteq\!\sim} \beta_9$
∞	$\alpha_{10} \sqsubseteq \beta_{10},\ \alpha_{11} \sqsubseteq \beta_{11},\ \alpha_{12} \sqsubseteq \beta_{12}$

Table 4.3: Exceptionality sequence

any exceptionality sequence but rather everything is taken into account to determine if a query in rationally entailed from a defeasible knowledge base. However, there are cases in which everything is thrown away, and all that remains are the classical statements (∞) and you still cannot get rid of the problematic cases.

To illustrate the main algorithm let us use Example 6 as our initial knowledge base and also use the derived knowledge base $\mathcal{K}^* = \mathcal{T}^* \cup \mathcal{D}^*$ and the exceptionality sequence $\mathcal{E}_0, \mathcal{E}_1, \ldots, \mathcal{E}_i$ to find out if Penguin $\mathbin{\sqsubseteq\!\sim}$ Wings is in the rational closure of $\mathcal{K}$. The RationalClosure algorithm will execute as follows.

1. The RationalClosure algorithm receives a knowledge base $\mathcal{K} = \mathcal{T} \cup \mathcal{D}$ and corresponding knowledge base $\mathcal{K}^* = \mathcal{T}^* \cup \mathcal{D}^*$, a an exceptionality sequence $\mathcal{E}_0, \ldots, \mathcal{E}_n$ and finally a query α. In this example the query is Penguin $\mathbin{\sqsubseteq\!\sim}$ Wings. The output is true if the query is rationally entailed from the knowledge or false otherwise.

2. Line 1 initialises a variable i to 0. The while-loop on line 2 checks if the materialisation of $\mathcal{E}$ with the conjunction of the antecedent (C) is subsumed by bottom $\perp$ as well as if i is less than n. If the statement evaluates to true, i is incremented by 1.

3. At this stage $\prod \overline{\mathcal{E}_0} = (\neg\text{Bird} \sqcup \text{Fly}) \sqcap (\neg\text{Bird} \sqcup \text{Wings}) \sqcap (\neg\text{Penguin} \sqcup \neg\text{Fly}) \sqcap$ Penguin $\sqsubseteq \perp$. Given this, we can check that $\mathcal{T}^* \models \prod \overline{\mathcal{E}_i} \sqcap C \sqsubseteq \perp$ i.e., $\{\text{Penguin} \sqsubseteq \text{Bird}, \text{Robin} \sqsubseteq \text{Bird}\} \models (\neg\text{Bird}\sqcup\text{Fly})\sqcap(\neg\text{Bird}\sqcup\text{Wings})\sqcap(\neg\text{Penguin}\sqcup \neg\text{Fly}) \sqcap$ Penguin $\sqsubseteq \perp$. This evaluates to true and the value of i is incremented to 1.

4. Next the condition in in while loop checks for $\mathcal{T}^* \models \prod \overline{\mathcal{E}_1} \sqcap C \sqsubseteq \perp$. That is $\{\text{Penguin} \sqsubseteq \text{Bird}, \text{Robin} \sqsubseteq \text{Bird}\} \models (\neg\text{Penguin} \sqcup \neg\text{Fly}) \sqcap$ Penguin $\sqsubseteq \perp$. This evaluates to false and the while loop terminates.

5. $i \leq n$ in line 4, so the body of the if statement executes.

6. Finally, using line 5 we see that $\mathcal{T}^* \not\models \prod \overline{\mathcal{E}_1} \sqcap C \sqsubseteq D$, i.e., $\{\text{Penguin} \sqsubseteq \text{Bird}, \text{Robin} \sqsubseteq \text{Bird}\} \not\models (\neg\text{Penguin} \sqcup \neg\text{Fly}) \sqcap$ Penguin $\sqsubseteq$ Wings. The program halts and returns `false`.

Table 4.4 represents the exceptionality sequence for Example 6 and illustrates a concrete example of the high level version of Table 4.3. The statements in $\mathcal{E}_0$ are thrown away as shown in step 3 above. More precisely anytime the while-loop condition evaluates to true what is essentially happening is that the algorithm is throwing away statements by moving from one level to the next until the condition evaluates to `false`. The action of moving from one level to the next is the algorithm throwing away statements that cause conflicts within the knowledge base.

$\mathcal{E}_0$	Bird $\mathrel{\vphantom{=}\sqsubseteq\mkern-14mu\raise2pt\hbox{$\scriptstyle\sim$}}$ Fly, Bird $\mathrel{\vphantom{=}\sqsubseteq\mkern-14mu\raise2pt\hbox{$\scriptstyle\sim$}}$ Wings, Penguin $\mathrel{\vphantom{=}\sqsubseteq\mkern-14mu\raise2pt\hbox{$\scriptstyle\sim$}}$ ¬Fly
$\mathcal{E}_1$	Penguin $\mathrel{\vphantom{=}\sqsubseteq\mkern-14mu\raise2pt\hbox{$\scriptstyle\sim$}}$ ¬Fly
∞	Penguin $\sqsubseteq$ Bird, Robin $\sqsubseteq$ Bird

Table 4.4: Exceptionality sequence for Example 6

4.4   Summary

In this chapter we discussed defeasible reasoning which allows us to handle exceptions in knowledge bases. We started by clarifying the difference between defeasible reasoning and non- monotonic reasoning. Thereafter described the various approaches to defeasible reasoning and then drilled down to a single approach which is applicable to our research.

We concluded the chapter by describing the rational closure algorithm which is the specific approach to defeasible reasoning that we use in this **book**.

Chapter 5

Defeasible Explanation

5.1   Overview

In this chapter we present our main contribution of the book which is an algorithm to compute justifications for defeasible knowledge bases.

In Chapter 2 we presented the foundations of classical description logics. We showed how we can represent information about a domain in a knowledge base and also make use of the knowledge base to infer useful information through entailment. Next in Chapter 3 we discussed and highlighted the importance of providing explanations for entailments that are derived from knowledge bases. By computing single and multiple justifications for entailments, users are able to easily understand entailments as well as debug and repair inconsistencies found in knowledge bases. Finally, in Chapter 4 we discussed the issue of handling exceptions when the information in our knowledge base presents a typical rather than strict relationship.

The chapter is organized as follows. We first present the problem of computing justifications for defeasible knowledge bases and then present an algorithm, then conclude the chapter by discussing extensions that can be made for defeasible explanations.

5.2   Extending Explanation to Defeasible Reasoning

In order to compute justifications in the classical case we need to first determine the minimal subsets that is sufficient for the entailment to hold. In Chapter 3 we saw that an entailment can have more than one justification, however not all justifications are correct and cannot be used to prove that a given entailment holds. This is because when computing justifications for classical description logics, contradictions in the knowledge base may arise and that means that certain justifications can not be used to prove an entailment.

We have seen from Chapter 4 that defeasibility adds an extra layer of complexity when computing entailment. The rational closure algorithm discussed in the previous chapter uses the Exceptional and ComputeRanking algorithms to determine which axioms are more exceptional in the context of the knowledge base.

However, we can still compute justifications for defeasible knowledge bases using minimal subsets because in Chapter 4 it was shown that defeasible statements are first ranked according to exceptionality and then are treated as classical statements through materialisation. Therefore, it is because we are turning them into classical statements that we can make use of minimal subsets. The only difference is that only some of those minimal subsets will be appropriate and applicable.

This is important because when inconsistencies or conflicts arise in the knowledge base, the axioms with the lowest ranking are discarded first because they are considered to be more general. This means that if a justification consists of axioms that have been discarded the entailment will no longer be inferable.

In other words, explanation in the classical case only requires that you extract the axioms that support the entailment. The challenge for the classical case is that they may be multiple explanations and how to get them efficiently. In the defeasible case some statements are more prone to be removed than others, thus the ranking is the starting point or the basis to build an explanation. Essentially axioms are still going to be selected from the knowledge base, however the way in which the axioms are selected is different from the classical case because we are constraining things according to the ranking of statements.

In order to make use of the ranking we need to first modify the definition of the **RationalClosure** algorithm given in Chapter 4 to give more information by returning the ranking at which execution halts. In other words return the exceptional sequence number (rank) which makes the condition in the while-loop false. The **RationalClosureForJustifications** algorithm is modified on lines 5 and 7 such that the algorithm returns `true`/`false` and a rank i.

Algorithm 5: RationalClosureForJustifications($\mathcal{K}$, α)

> **Input:** $\mathcal{K} = \mathcal{T} \cup \mathcal{D}$, the corresponding $\mathcal{K}^* = \mathcal{T}^* \cup \mathcal{D}^*$, the sequence $\mathcal{E}_0, \ldots, \mathcal{E}_n$,
> and a query $\alpha = C \mathrel{\reflectbox{$\precsim$}} D$.
> **Output:** `true` if $\mathcal{K} \vdash_{\mathsf{rat}} C \mathrel{\reflectbox{$\precsim$}} D$, `false` otherwise and a rank i

1   $i \leftarrow 0$

2   **while** $\mathcal{T}^* \models \prod \overline{\mathcal{E}_i} \sqcap C \sqsubseteq \bot$ *and* $i \leq n$ **do**

3     $\lfloor \quad i \quad i+1$

4   **if** $i \leq n$ **then**

5     $\lfloor$ **return** $\mathcal{T}^* \models \prod \overline{\mathcal{E}_i} \sqcap C \sqsubseteq D$, i

6   **else**

7     $\lfloor$ **return** $\mathcal{T}^* \models C \sqsubseteq D$, i

---

By combining the rational closure algorithm to handle defeasible knowledge bases and the algorithms to compute justifications we provide a framework to compute explanations for defeasible reasoning.

The algorithm to compute justifications for defeasible knowledge bases for an entailment η is summarised as follows: it uses **RationalClosure** and **ComputeAllJustifications** as sub-procedures. The first step is to compute whether or not the query is rationally entailed from the knowledge base and return the rank at which the rational closure was determined. The rank is central in determining justifications for defeasible knowledge bases because it indicates which layers have been discarded.

Before we provide a detailed description of the algorithm using some example queries consider Figure 5.1 which illustrates how the exceptionality sequences are used do compute justifications. The basic idea is that once the rank is retrieved

---

Algorithm 6: ComputeDefeasibleJustifications($\mathcal{K}, \eta$)

 Input: $\mathcal{K} = \mathcal{T} \cup \mathcal{D}$, the corresponding $\mathcal{K}^* = \mathcal{T}^* \cup \mathcal{D}^*$, the sequence $\mathcal{E}_0, \ldots, \mathcal{E}_n$,
   the ranking $R = \mathcal{D}_0, \ldots, \mathcal{D}_n$, and a query $\eta = C \mathbin{\vphantom{\sqsubseteq}\sqsubset\!\sim} D$.

 Output: Justification $\mathcal{J}$

1   $i \leftarrow 0$

2   $\mathcal{J}_{result} \leftarrow \emptyset$

3   $rank \leftarrow$ RationalClosureForJustifications($\mathcal{K}, R, \eta$)

4   **if** $rank = 0$ **then**

5    $\mathcal{J}_{result} \leftarrow$ ComputeAllJustifications($\mathcal{K}, \eta$)

6   **return** J_{result}

7   **while** $i < rank$ **do**

8    $\mathcal{K}_{new} \leftarrow \mathcal{K}_{new} \setminus \mathcal{D}_i$

9    $i \quad i + 1$

10   $\mathcal{J}_{result} \leftarrow$ ComputeAllJustifications($\mathcal{K}_{new}, \eta$)

11   **return** $\mathcal{J}_{result}$

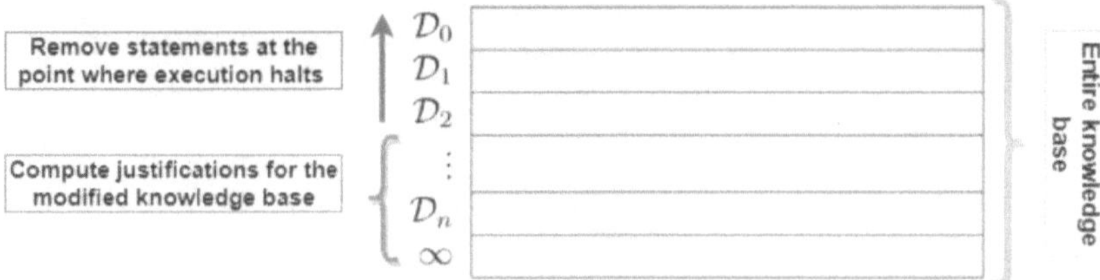

Figure 5.1: Computation of justifications for a defeasible knowledge base

we no longer consider the statements that are part of the exceptionality sequences above. For example if a rank of 2 is retrieved, the statements contained in $\mathcal{E}_0$ and $\mathcal{E}_1$ are removed and only the statements below $\mathcal{E}_2$ will be used to compute justifications.

Example 7 To illustrate the algorithm to compute justifications for defeasible knowledge bases, consider example 2 from Chapter 3. Note that rather than using the classical definition of the knowledge base we represent the information using the defeasible case. Given $\mathcal{K} = (\mathcal{T}, \mathcal{D})$

$$\mathcal{T} = \left\{ \begin{array}{c} \text{Penguin} \sqsubseteq \text{Bird}, \\ \text{Robin} \sqsubseteq \text{Bird} \\ \text{SpecialPenguin} \sqsubseteq \text{Penguin} \end{array} \right\}$$

$$\mathcal{D} = \left\{ \begin{array}{c} \text{Bird} \mathbin{\vphantom{\sqsubseteq}\sqsubset\!\sim} \text{Fly}, \\ \text{Bird} \mathbin{\vphantom{\sqsubseteq}\sqsubset\!\sim} \text{Wings}, \\ \text{Penguin} \mathbin{\vphantom{\sqsubseteq}\sqsubset\!\sim} \neg\text{Fly} \\ \text{SpecialPenguin} \mathbin{\vphantom{\sqsubseteq}\sqsubset\!\sim} \text{Fly} \end{array} \right\}$$

Using the knowledge base above we shall show how the algorithm will handle the following queries:

(i) Robin $\mathbin{\vphantom{\sqsubseteq}\sqsubset\!\sim}$ Wings

(ii) $\mathsf{Penguin} \mathrel{\sqsubseteq\mkern-10mu\sim} \mathsf{Wings}$

(iii) $\mathsf{SpecialPenguin} \mathrel{\sqsubseteq\mkern-10mu\sim} \mathsf{Fly}$

To make things easier the corresponding exceptionality sequence and ranking sequence for the knowledge base above is given in Table 5.1 and Table 5.2 respectively using the ComputeRanking algorithm defined in Chapter 4.

The exceptionality sequence is mainly used to compute the rational closure of a query and retrieve the rank number whereas the ranking sequence is used to determine which portion of the knowledge base will be used to compute the justifications.

$\mathcal{E}_0$	$\mathsf{Bird} \mathrel{\sqsubseteq\mkern-10mu\sim} \mathsf{Fly}, \mathsf{Bird} \mathrel{\sqsubseteq\mkern-10mu\sim} \mathsf{Wings}, \mathsf{Penguin} \mathrel{\sqsubseteq\mkern-10mu\sim} \neg\mathsf{Fly}, \mathsf{SpecialPenguin} \mathrel{\sqsubseteq\mkern-10mu\sim} \mathsf{Fly}$
$\mathcal{E}_1$	$\mathsf{Penguin} \mathrel{\sqsubseteq\mkern-10mu\sim} \neg\mathsf{Fly}, \mathsf{SpecialPenguin} \mathrel{\sqsubseteq\mkern-10mu\sim} \mathsf{Fly}$
$\mathcal{E}_2$	$\mathsf{SpecialPenguin} \mathrel{\sqsubseteq\mkern-10mu\sim} \mathsf{Fly}$
∞	$\mathsf{Penguin} \sqsubseteq \mathsf{Bird}, \mathsf{Robin} \sqsubseteq \mathsf{Bird}, \mathsf{SpecialPenguin} \sqsubseteq \mathsf{Penguin}$

Table 5.1: The exceptionality sequence for $\mathcal{K}$

$\mathcal{D}_0$	$\mathsf{Bird} \mathrel{\sqsubseteq\mkern-10mu\sim} \mathsf{Fly}, \mathsf{Bird} \mathrel{\sqsubseteq\mkern-10mu\sim} \mathsf{Wings}$
$\mathcal{D}_1$	$\mathsf{Penguin} \mathrel{\sqsubseteq\mkern-10mu\sim} \neg\mathsf{Fly}$
$\mathcal{D}_2$	$\mathsf{SpecialPenguin} \mathrel{\sqsubseteq\mkern-10mu\sim} \mathsf{Fly}$
∞	$\mathsf{Penguin} \sqsubseteq \mathsf{Bird}, \mathsf{Robin} \sqsubseteq \mathsf{Bird}, \mathsf{SpecialPenguin} \sqsubseteq \mathsf{Penguin}$

Table 5.2: Ranking sequence for $\mathcal{K}$

For $\eta = \mathsf{Robin} \mathrel{\sqsubseteq\mkern-10mu\sim} \mathsf{Wings}$ the algorithm executes as follows:

1. The ComputeDefeasibleJustifications algorithm receives a knowledge base $\mathcal{K} = \mathcal{T} \cup \mathcal{D}$ and corresponding knowledge base $\mathcal{K}^* = \mathcal{T}^* \cup \mathcal{D}^*$, the sequence $\mathcal{E}_0, \ldots, \mathcal{E}_n$, the ranking $R = \mathcal{D}_0, \ldots, \mathcal{D}_n$ which are a collection of sets of sentences and finally a query η. The output is a set $\mathcal{J}$ that contains the justifications for the query η.

2. Line 1 initialises a variable i to 0 and a set $\mathcal{J}_{result}$ is initialised to an empty set on line 2.

3. On line 3 we retrieve the rank at which the rational closure algorithm terminates. For our algorithm we use the modified version of the RationalClosure algorithm.

4. If the rank is equal to 0. Compute the justifications for the entire knowledge base and return the justification set. (Lines 4-6).

5. If rank is greater than 0, the while-loop on line 7-9 removes axioms contained in ranking sequence 0 to rank minus 1.

6. On line 10 we compute all the justifications for the query η and assign it to a variable $\mathcal{J}_{result}$. This is a set which contains justifications in the form $\mathcal{J}_{result} = \{\mathcal{J}_1, \mathcal{J}_2, \mathcal{J}_3, \ldots, \mathcal{J}_n\}$

7. For η = Robin $\mathrel{\vcenter{\hbox{$\sim$}}\mkern-14mu\raise3pt\hbox{$\sqsubset$}}$ Wings a rank of 0 is returned thus the justifications are computed using the entire knowledge base. See Figure 5.2 for an illustration of which portion of the the knowledge base is considered.

8. Thus, the final answer is the justification set $\mathcal{J}_{result} = \{\mathcal{J}_1\}$ where $\mathcal{J}_1 = \{$Robin $\sqsubseteq$ Bird, Bird $\mathrel{\vcenter{\hbox{$\sim$}}\mkern-14mu\raise3pt\hbox{$\sqsubset$}}$ Wings$\}$

$\mathcal{D}_0$	Bird $\mathrel{\vcenter{\hbox{$\sim$}}\mkern-14mu\raise3pt\hbox{$\sqsubset$}}$ Fly, Bird $\mathrel{\vcenter{\hbox{$\sim$}}\mkern-14mu\raise3pt\hbox{$\sqsubset$}}$ Wings	
$\mathcal{D}_1$	Penguin $\mathrel{\vcenter{\hbox{$\sim$}}\mkern-14mu\raise3pt\hbox{$\sqsubset$}}$ ¬Fly	Entire knowledge base
$\mathcal{D}_2$	SpecialPenguin $\mathrel{\vcenter{\hbox{$\sim$}}\mkern-14mu\raise3pt\hbox{$\sqsubset$}}$ Fly	
∞	Penguin $\sqsubseteq$ Bird, Robin $\sqsubseteq$ Bird, SpecialPenguin $\sqsubseteq$ Penguin	

Figure 5.2: Computation of justifications for query 1

This illustrates how the justifications will be computed when a rank number of zero is returned. In other words when the query and the knowledge base do not result in conflicts and no statements need to be discarded.

For the next query η = Penguin $\mathrel{\vcenter{\hbox{$\sim$}}\mkern-14mu\raise3pt\hbox{$\sqsubset$}}$ Wings the algorithm executes as follows:

1. The ComputeDefeasibleJustifications algorithm receives a knowledge base $\mathcal{K} = \mathcal{T} \cup \mathcal{D}$ and corresponding knowledge base $\mathcal{K}^* = \mathcal{T}^* \cup \mathcal{D}^*$, the sequence $\mathcal{E}_0, \dots, \mathcal{E}_n$, the ranking $R = \mathcal{D}_0, \dots, \mathcal{D}_n$ which are a collection of sets of sentences and finally a query η. The output is a set $\mathcal{J}$ that contains the justifications for the query η.

2. Line 1 initialises a variable i to 0 and a set $\mathcal{J}_{result}$ is initialised to an empty set on line 2.

3. On line 3 we retrieve the rank at which the rational closure algorithm terminates using the modified version of the RationalClosure algorithm.

4. For η = Penguin $\mathrel{\vcenter{\hbox{$\sim$}}\mkern-14mu\raise3pt\hbox{$\sqsubset$}}$ Wings a rank of 2 is returned thus the justifications are computed using a subset of the knowledge base as shown in Figure 5.3.

5. The If-statement block on lines 4-6 are skipped since rank is greater than 0.

6. Next the while-loop on lines 7-9 removes axioms contained in ranking sequence $\mathcal{D}_0$ and $\mathcal{D}_1$.

7. On line 10 we compute all the justifications for the query η and assign it to a variable $\mathcal{J}_{result}$. In this case $\mathcal{J}_{result} = \emptyset$

$\mathcal{D}_0$	~~Bird $\mathrel{\vcenter{\hbox{$\sim$}}\mkern-14mu\raise3pt\hbox{$\sqsubset$}}$ Fly, Bird $\mathrel{\vcenter{\hbox{$\sim$}}\mkern-14mu\raise3pt\hbox{$\sqsubset$}}$ Wings~~	
$\mathcal{D}_1$	~~Penguin $\mathrel{\vcenter{\hbox{$\sim$}}\mkern-14mu\raise3pt\hbox{$\sqsubset$}}$ ¬Fly~~	
$\mathcal{D}_2$	SpecialPenguin $\mathrel{\vcenter{\hbox{$\sim$}}\mkern-14mu\raise3pt\hbox{$\sqsubset$}}$ Fly	New knowledge base
∞	Penguin $\sqsubseteq$ Bird, Robin $\sqsubseteq$ Bird, SpecialPenguin $\sqsubseteq$ Penguin	

Figure 5.3: Computation of justifications for query 2

The argument why $\mathcal{J}_{result} = \emptyset$ is that the axioms required to prove that the possible justification $\mathcal{J} = \{\mathsf{Penguin} \sqsubseteq \mathsf{Bird}, \mathsf{Bird} \mathrel{\sqsubseteq\mkern-10mu\sim} \mathsf{Wings}\}$ have been discarded. This is because Penguins are exceptional cases thus, the axioms in the first level are removed. Since $\mathsf{Bird} \mathrel{\sqsubseteq\mkern-10mu\sim} \mathsf{Wings}$ is discarded we cannot conclude anymore that Penguins have wings. This information can be used to build an explanation to prove why $\mathcal{K} \not\models \mathsf{Penguin} \sqsubseteq \mathsf{Wings}$ and is more complicated when compared to explanations for the classical case.

The final query $\eta = \mathsf{SpecialPenguin} \mathrel{\sqsubseteq\mkern-10mu\sim} \mathsf{Fly}$ executes as follows:

1. The $\mathsf{ComputeDefeasibleJustifications}$ algorithm receives a knowledge base $\mathcal{K} = \mathcal{T} \cup \mathcal{D}$ and corresponding knowledge base $\mathcal{K}^* = \mathcal{T}^* \cup \mathcal{D}^*$, the sequence $\mathcal{E}_0, \ldots, \mathcal{E}_n$, the ranking $R = \mathcal{D}_0, \ldots, \mathcal{D}_n$ which are a collection of sets of sentences and finally a query η. The output is a set $\mathcal{J}$ that contains the justifications for the query η.

2. Line 1 initialises a variable i to 0 and a set $\mathcal{J}_{result}$ is initialised to an empty set on line 2.

3. On line 3 we retrieve a rank of 2 using the modified version of the $\mathsf{RationalClosure}$ algorithm .

4. The If-statement block on lines 4-6 are skipped since rank is greater than 0.

5. Next the while-loop on lines 7-9 removes axioms contained in ranking sequence $\mathcal{D}_0$ and $\mathcal{D}_1$. Refer to Figure 5.4 to see which portion of the knowledge is used o compute the justifications.

6. On line 10 we compute all the justifications for the query η and assign it to a variable $\mathcal{J}_{result}$. In this case $\mathcal{J}_{result} = \mathcal{J}_1$

7. Thus, the final answer is the justification set $\mathcal{J}_{result} = \{\mathcal{J}_1\}$ where $\mathcal{J}_1 = \{\mathsf{SpecialPenguin} \mathrel{\sqsubseteq\mkern-10mu\sim} \mathsf{Fly}\}$

$\mathcal{D}_0$	$\mathsf{Bird} \mathrel{\sqsubseteq\mkern-10mu\sim} \mathsf{Fly}, \mathsf{Bird} \mathrel{\sqsubseteq\mkern-10mu\sim} \mathsf{Wings}$	
$\mathcal{D}_1$	$\mathsf{Penguin} \mathrel{\sqsubseteq\mkern-10mu\sim} \mathsf{Fly}$	
$\mathcal{D}_2$	$\mathsf{SpecialPenguin} \mathrel{\sqsubseteq\mkern-10mu\sim} \mathsf{Fly}$	New knowledge base
∞	$\mathsf{Penguin} \sqsubseteq \mathsf{Bird}, \mathsf{Robin} \sqsubseteq \mathsf{Bird}, \mathsf{SpecialPenguin} \sqsubseteq \mathsf{Penguin}$	

Figure 5.4: Computation of justifications for query 3

Looking at the $\mathsf{ComputeDefeasibleJustifications}$ algorithm description above, we now return to Example 2 given in Chapter 3. Recall that using the knowledge base defined in Example 2 there are 2 minimal subsets (justifications) that support the query $\mathsf{SpecialPenguin} \sqsubseteq \mathsf{Fly}$ i.e., special penguins can fly.

$\mathcal{J}_1 = \{ \mathsf{SpecialPenguin} \mathrel{\sqsubseteq\mkern-10mu\sim} \mathsf{Fly} \}$

$\mathcal{J}_2 = \{ \mathsf{SpecialPenguin} \sqsubseteq \mathsf{Penguin}, \mathsf{Penguin} \sqsubseteq \mathsf{Bird}, \mathsf{Bird} \mathrel{\sqsubseteq\mkern-10mu\sim} \mathsf{Fly} \}$

However, the only valid justification that supports the query is $\mathcal{J}_1$ because when we rewrite the knowledge base in Example 2 to its corresponding defeasible version. The axioms that are required to make $\mathcal{J}_2$ valid are discarded using the

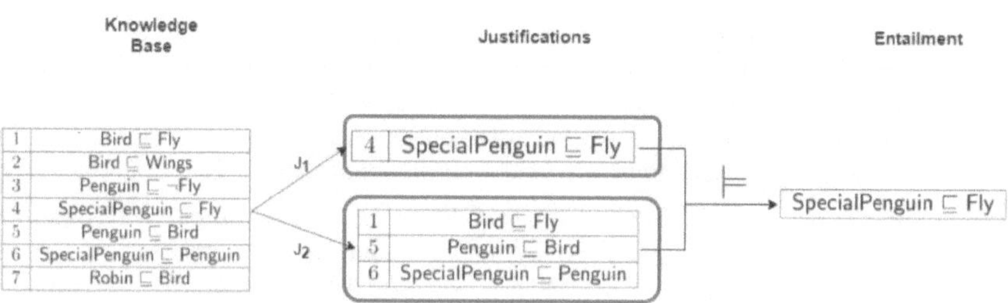

Figure 5.5: Multiple justifications for an entailment from the original knowledge base

ComputeDefeasibleJustifications algorithm described above, thus proving that justification $\mathcal{J}_1$ is the only true justification for the given knowledge base and query.

Since the algorithm used to compute justifications for defeasible knowledge bases relies on two separate algorithms, the computational complexity to retrieve all justifications depends on the expressiveness of the description logic. In this case, the algorithm to compute rational entailment is no higher than that of computing entailment in the underlying classical DL. Additionally, the experiments conducted by Horridge [26] on naturally occurring knowledge bases also indicate that computation of all justifications, even though extremely large, halts because usually a subset of the knowledge base is considered. This is expected to be the case with defeasible knowledge bases because we do not consider those statements beyond the rank returned from the rational closure algorithm or the point where conflicts arise.

This approach of handling justifications for defeasible knowledge bases is attractive because it starts by identifying the preference of statements within a knowledge base. Computation of exceptionality is done first and then ranking of statements. Meaning, whenever there is a conflict, it is easy to handle by simply looking at the exceptionality of statements. Additionally, it has already been established by Britz et al [12] that their algorithm is semantically intuitive as well as computationally inexpensive. Thus, these two properties are good conditions to compute justifications in this manner.

5.3   English Explanations for Defeasible Entailment

Another area of interest that has been briefly mentioned is using justifications as a foundation for natural languages explanations. Using a natural language such as English, it becomes easier to understand and interpret entailments. Translation to natural languages are out of the scope of this book but is worth mentioning because it is of great value. Natural language explanations will enable users who do not need to have a logic background to understand what is going on when computing defeasible entailment.

To make this point more clear, in order to appreciate and understand how justifications are derived for defeasible knowledge bases users need to first have some basic background or understanding of logics. Next they need to be knowledgeable on defeasible reasoning and how exceptionality and the ranking of statements fit together. Or at least be able to conceptualize this notion of ranks, layers or levels been discarded which is not as easy and requires time.

Providing the justifications is a good starting point because the state which axioms are responsible for a given entailment. However, users still need to connect the axioms together to make sense out of them . Thus providing explanations in form of sentences or 'story-line' will make entailments more understandable. For example for the query $\eta = \mathsf{SpecialPenguin} \mathrel{\vcenter{\hbox{$\subsetneq$}}\!\!\sim} \mathsf{Fly}$, the following might be a possible explanation why $\mathsf{SpecialPenguin} \mathrel{\vcenter{\hbox{$\subsetneq$}}\!\!\sim} \mathsf{Fly}$ is the only valid justification.

"Although we have 2 minimal subsets $(\mathcal{J}_1,\ \mathcal{J}_2)$ that support the entailment. Only $\mathcal{J}_1$ is valid because to get the conclusion that special penguins usually fly we had to discard statements that are necessary to make $\mathcal{J}_2$ valid".

5.4   Summary

In this chapter we presented an algorithm to compute justifications for defeasible entailment. In the first section we explained why a modified version of the rational closure algorithm was required in order to retrieve more information to compute justifications. Specifically we need the rank number at which the rational closure terminates.

The rank number is used to determine which portion of the knowledge base will be used to compute justifications when there are conflicts within the knowledge base and we illustrated this using three different queries.

The last section of the chapter gave a brief motivation why extending this **book** to natural language explanations is important.

Chapter 6

Conclusion and Future Work

This chapter is composed of two sections. The first section provides a comprehensive overview of the research which we discussed throughout this **book** and the second section concludes the chapter with a discussion on some open questions and issues about explanations for defeasible entailment.

6.1 Summary of Contribution

The main contribution of this **book** is extending justification-based explanations to defeasible reasoning. Specifically, providing justifications for the description logics $\mathcal{ALC}$ that uses rational closure as the defeasible reasoning framework.

We first introduced the basic description logic $\mathcal{ALC}$ for knowledge representation in Chapter 2. We highlighted some description logics reasoning services and discussed how entailment (logical consequence) can be used to derive implicit information from our knowledge base.

Chapter 3 built on the foundations given in Chapter 2 and showed how justifications are useful in terms of understanding entailments that are derived from a knowledge base. Additionally, we highlighted why justifications are the most common form of explanations and also discussed the algorithms that compute them.

Next we addressed the issue of handling exceptions in $\mathcal{ALC}$ knowledge bases in Chapter 4. We started by clarifying the differences between defeasible reasoning and non- monotonic reasoning. Thereafter described the various approaches to defeasible reasoning and then drilled down to a single approach which is rational closure.

Finally, we concluded the **book** by describing the algorithm to compute justifications for defeasible knowledge bases. It was shown that in order to accurately derive justifications for situations where a knowledge base may contain conflicting information, we need to establish the point at which conflicts arise i.e., determine the rank. The rank can then be used to remove axioms that are causing conflicts and then computation of justifications are calculated for the new knowledge base.

The work done in this **book** is based on the work proposed by Britz et al [12] This is of great importance because compared to other frameworks such as the one by Casini and Straccia [21] which lacks an appropriate semantics, the syntax presented for defeasible subsumption has an appropriate semantics that is intuitive. Furthermore, the derived algorithm to compute rational entailment can be reduced to classical entailment checking meaning its computational complexity is no worse than that of entailment checking in the classical underlying DL.

6.2   Open Issues and Future Work

At this stage there are four distinct paths for future work available for justification-based explanations for defeasible reasoning.

To begin with, an implementation and testing of the ComputeDefeasibleJustifications algorithm is required. A good starting point is to create a plugin for the ontology editor Protégé which has an implementation for rational closure.

The next avenue to explore is the possibility of extending justifications to the other forms of defeasible reasoning within the KLM approach. Since rational closure falls under the umbrella of the preferential approach to defeasible reasoning it seems reasonable to conclude that similar extensions can be made for the entire class of defeasible entailment relations. For example lexicographic closure [20] and relevant closure [14] are other forms of defeasible entailment relations within the class but differ in the number of conclusions that can be drawn from a knowledge base.

The third open issue that can be looked into is a theoretical understanding of explanation for other non-monotonic reasoning frameworks. The description of justification-based explanations provided in this **book** works because of the way in which rational closure algorithm is structured. That is, we can take the defeasible statements and transform to classical statements and then compute the justifica-tions. Other forms of non-monotonic reasoning such as circumscription and default logic also perform defeasible entailment and it will be a good idea to know how defeasible explanation works for them.

The final issue for future consideration is to extend justification-based explanations to natural language explanations to assist users in understanding entailments. Explainable AI is a relevant research area and this **book** can serve as a starting point to serve this purpose.